MADONNA OR COURTESAN?

The Jewish Woman in Christian Literature

To My Mother
A Most Remarkable Jewish Woman

MADONNA OR COURTESAN?

The Jewish Woman in Christian Literature

LIVIA BITTON-JACKSON

The Seabury Press / New York

1982
The Seabury Press
815 Second Avenue
New York, N.Y. 10017

Printed in the United States of America

Acknowledgments

Years of thought and passionate effort are woven into the fabric of this book. Miles of search for literary sources, supported by a grant from the City University of New York PSC-CUNY Research Award Program, took me to the major libraries of London, Paris, Madrid, Munich, and Jerusalem. The zealous identification with Jewish destiny of my son, M. Avinoam the idealist, and the sensitivity of my daughter, Emly the poet, provided inspiration. The loving encouragement of my husband, Len Jackson, gave sorely needed self-confidence. The scholarly guidance of my friend, Arthur Beringause, served as initial support. But, most of all, it was the keen eye and unflagging faith of my editor, Molly McConnell, that made the emergence of the manuscript into a book possible. I hope all of them will derive pleasure and perhaps even pride from this book.

Library of Congress Cataloging in Publication Data
Jackson, Livia Bitton.
The mystique of Jewish woman in Chrishtian literature.

Bibliography: p.
1. Women, Jewish, in literature. I. Title.
PN56.3.J4J3 1982 809'.93352042 82-10750
ISBN 0-8164-2440-3 (pbk.)

Contents

Introduction

Myth of the Wandering Jewess

> The history of this one family is the history of the whole human race! Passing through what innumerable generations, running through the veins of the poor and the rich, of the robber and the sovereign, of the sage and the idiot, of the hero and the dastard, of the saint and the atheist, has not my sister's blood been perpetuated in this very hour![1]

Her name is Herodias, and she is the eternal Wandering Jewess, mother of mankind. This is Eugène Sue's interpretation of the famous myth: the Wandering Jewess is like Eve from whose womb issues the human race. But unlike the primal biblical mother, Herodias is immortal, and through a succession of lives follows the fortunes of her offspring, shielding the weak and admonishing the powerful.

Sue's version is but one in a body of literature that has evolved about this fascinating figure of myth. In some literary works she is an irresistible seductress, a she-demon cajoling men into submission. In others, she is a saint who suffers silently the anguish of mankind, and toils with unwavering faith for its salvation. In most, she is humanity's only hope of redemption in the midst of despair. As in Karl Gutzkow's discourse on the "Eternal Jewess" (1868), she is the manifestation of all the mythical women in all cultures. She is all the good fairies and the bad fairies in one. She is Egyptian Pharaïldis from which such antithetical figures as the German Frau Hulden, or Frau

Hölle, and the French Fée Aboude were derived. Frau Hölle is the embodiment of carnal sin and is identified with the Wild Huntswoman of the German folktale, while Fée Aboude is a good fairy who seems to embody the kindness of woman.

The eternal Wandering Jewess stands for all women. All the spirited, passionate, and compassionate women of history may be seen as multiple representations of this single, central ideal. She is the spirit that moved Zenobia, the queen of Palmyra, Joan of Arc, Mary Stuart, Empress Theodora, Diane of Poitiers, Christina of Sweden, Pauline Bonaparte, Mme. de Staël, and others.

The Wandering Jewess is a figure of dichotomy. Primarily Woman, she is also unmistakably Jewess—in her allure, her effect, and especially her fate.

As Woman, whether angel of mercy or demon of desire, she is placed on a pedestal fashioned out of isolation and lack of understanding. She is womanhood resented, pampered, admired, and feared—but, most of all, misunderstood. Her aspirations, struggles, failures, virtues, and hopes have remained a mystery throughout the ages.

As Jewess, she is a symbol of the mystic omnipotence ascribed to Jews in legend and literature. This mystic power is mostly evil but even its good manifestations are frightening to innocent mortals. Myths of Jews as evil forces manipulating mankind are born of ignorance and misunderstanding. Ignorance of Jews, their faith and customs, bred the fear and prejudice out of which the mythical Jew emerged.

Such myth-making, unlike that of primitive men, is a substitute for an attempt to understand. At best a sign of ignorance and cowardice, more often it is a sign of emotional dishonesty. Myths transformed into stereotyped literary images have shaped attitudes toward women and toward Jews throughout the ages, causing both untold suffering. Women have been locked into roles that conformed to mythical preconceptions rather than reality. Myths have damned Jews and condemned them to a history of persecutions and massacres. Myths have distorted the Jew's image and prevented a natural flow of human communication with his Christian neighbors. Myths made the catastrophe of the Holocaust possible.

As the age-old mechanics of anti-Semitism, the myth-making process is investigated in this book through a literary-historical study, with the Jewish woman as its focal point. To eliminate interracial, interreligious and international hatreds, it is necessary to examine the origins of prejudice and the nature of its manipulation. An awareness of myths is an important first step. Sensitivity to stereotyping is another. This book is an attempt to foster the awareness and develop the sensitivity needed to prevent those distortions of facts that lead one human being to become the perpetrator of injustice, and another, its victim. By examining the historical-literary evidence of myth-making and its outcome, using stereotyped images of the Jewish woman in literature, this book endeavors to shed light also on the deceptive nature of the myth-making process and its dangers.

The Wandering Jewess is a most versatile myth. It has been adapted to many issues—political, religious, social—and it encompasses contradictory attitudes toward Jews as both good and evil. In this respect the Wandering Jewess is a unique, atypical image: she combines the stereotyped figures of the Jewish male and female, the figure of the sinister, evil Jew and the sweet, kind Jewess. Even her most frequently used names, Herodias or Salome, imply feminine wiles, ambition, and the power of seduction alongside virtues explicit in the narrative. Who is this wonderwoman, this mysterious Jewish mother of mankind?

Like her prototype Eve, who sprang from the body of Adam, the eternal Wandering Jewess is an outgrowth of the eternal Wandering Jew. She is, however, centuries younger than that figure of medieval legend who until the eighteenth century wandered womanless on the face of the earth. The "Age of Reason" created a feminine counterpart to the shadowy figure, and the fascinating myth of the Wandering Jewess was born.

The Wandering Jew himself materialized out of medieval fear and superstition. Pilgrims at the monastery of Ferrara reported in 1223 that they "had seen a certain Jew in Armenia who had been present at the Passion of the Lord, and, as He was going to His martyrdom, drove him along wickedly with these words, 'Go, go thou tempter and seducer, to receive what you have earned.' Jesus is said to have answered him: 'I go, and you will await me until I come again.' " This report, incorporated into a Bolognese chronicle for that year,[2] became the kernel of the myth that was to mushroom throughout centuries in Europe, England, and even America.

Five years later the Wandering Jew had acquired the name Cartaphilus and several fascinating qualities, among them the mystical mechanics of immortality: he was believed to grow old till the age of one hundred years and then return to age thirty in a continuous cycle of rejuvenation and a constant state of penitence, till the Second Coming.[3]

A preoccupation with Old Testament heroes in Reformation drama and literature lent a new dimension to the popular image of the Jew. His villainous features as Christ-killer, Judas, ritual child-murderer and usurer were now invested with an aura of mystery. The Jew was seen as an obscure figure from a distant land, sinister and ominous yet awesomely fascinating. But of this new fascination, combined with old fears, came the mythical figure as he entered the literature of the seventeenth century.

The Wandering Jew thus evolved was a tall, lanky man with long hair and enormous penetrating eyes. He was said to appear suddenly, unexpectedly, at the outskirts of villages and towns and then vanish again into thin air. News of his appearance would stir excitement and panic: he was believed to bring natural disasters—famine, floods, epidemics—or herald the end of the world.

The Wandering Jew of these accounts had had a wife and child whom he was compelled to abandon at the onset of his wandering. Thus the woman had not yet entered the legend. The first bona fide Wandering Woman, or Jewess, is sighted in 1743 by a German housewife, Frau Krüger, from the village of Helfte, who recorded the experience in a unique manuscript.[4]

In the Krüger account she was the daughter of a local Jew, Schmul Ner Ruhlmann, and she married the Wandering Jew. After the nuptials, attended by Frau Krüger, the couple took off for their wandering. Despite her admiration for them, Frau Krüger believed the Wandering couple exercised a disturbing effect on Christian morality.

Shortly after this, two conflicting versions of the Wandering Jewess myth appeared in Ukrainian folklore. In one tale she is the deceased daughter of the legendary Jew who sinned against Jesus. Immediately after the curse is pronounced upon him, the Jew goes to her grave and weeps. Arising from her coffin, she calls to him: "Faithless father! You are faithless toward God and faithless toward me; you don't deserve to cry on my grave." But he continues to weep and lament that God has taken her away so young. Then, he departs, to begin his everlasting wandering. In the second tale, the Jewess is an accomplice of the sinning Jew. She joins her man in chasing away Jesus from their doorstep and, sharing the curse, she roams the earth together with him.[5]

In the nineteenth century the Wandering Jewess becomes for the first time a dramatic heroine. In Edgar Quinet's morality play, *Ahasuerus* (1833), she is Rachel, a divinely beautiful fallen angel cast out of heaven for having taken pity on Ahasuerus. On earth she becomes a representative of ideal love, eternal faith, consolation and hope. She is an angel in human form whose divine purity and goodness on earth serve as man's salvation. Rachel is to complement Ahasuerus, the symbol of humanity, the embodiment of doubt, materialism and suffering. The two meet, fall in love and marry, then set out together on an endless journey through time. World events rush by them till the universe approaches a total collapse.

The final scene is the Day of Last Judgment. Ahasuerus, the center of a devastated, disintegrated universe, stands before the Judge—Christ. He has been abandoned by every element in Nature, everything has lost faith in him. His sentence depends on his ability to have inspired faith in others throughout his long sojourn. All is silent, however. Except one voice, the voice of Rachel's unwavering faith. "That voice has saved thee, Ahasuerus," intones Christ at the conclusion of the play. Sinful mankind cannot hope for salvation without the Woman-Redeemer. Her faith is humanity's hope.

Quinet's Rachel appeared with more pronounced Christian overtones a year later in P.F.C. Merville and J. de Maillan's *drame fantastique, Le Juif Errant* (*The Wandering Jew,* 1834). Here, her name is Esther and she is the daughter, not the wife, of Ahasuerus.

A succession of scenes depicts Esther's fate in various historical periods—from Judea during the Roman occupation to Versailles in the reign of Louis XV. Ever in jeopardy or flight from men's lust, Esther escapes at last by committing suicide—only to fall victim to the ultimate seducer: beyond death, Satan claims her soul.

The last act takes place in Hell. Ahasuerus gambles for his daughter's soul and succeeds in regaining it: an archangel transports the pure soul to heaven. In the epilogue, Esther reappears with an olive branch in her hand, and reveals to the astounded Ahasuerus the secret of his salvation: he has to humiliate himself before the tomb of Christ and touch the stone with faith. The promise of redemption is clear in her parting words: "Adieu, my father, I shall await you at the gate of Paradise." And so woman once again works the salvation of mankind.

Eugène Sue's *The Wandering Jew* (1844-45) introduces a new concept in the Wandering Jew-Jewess myth. He is the sufferer, champion of the oppressed, and she, his sister, is the biological mother of the oppressed. Like Eve, the "mother of all living," the Wandering Jewess is the cause and the cure of human pain. Ahasuerus' and Herodias' struggle for humanity is their raison d'être. The Jew, because it is his mission; the Jewess, because mankind is the issue of her womb.

The popularity of the Wandering Jewess theme no doubt accounts for its use in less exalted contexts, as well. In Ceferino Tressera's political pro-Huguenot novel, *La Judia Errante* (1889), the Jewess is a clever secret agent smuggling important documents. In Christopher Kuffner's novel of social criticism, *Die ewige Jüdin und der Orang-Outang* (1846), the Eternal Jewess carries on a conversation about social problems with an orangoutang. And in Joseph P. Heywood's dramatic poem, "Salome" (1867), the heroine is biblical Salome pursued by an endless succession of men, whom she travels all over the globe to escape—hence the epithet "Wandering"!

In *Salome, the Wandering Jewess: My First Two Thousand Years of Love (1931),* a satire on woman suffrage, George S. Viereck and Paul Eldridge ridicule feminist ambitions through the image of the eternal Wandering Jewess, a capricious, overbearing, willful, destructive and frustrated amazon. The power of seduction inherent in the New Testament heroine and the ambitious passion inherent in the Wild Huntswoman of the German tale are both manifested in this formidable female.

As a punishment for her share in the execution of John the Baptist, this Salome is condemned to an endless succession of lives—an unfair imposition on mankind. For Salome, far from suffering at the thought of eternal life, resolves to conquer man and the moon. By man she means all males of the human species, and by the moon, the planet which keeps women in arbitrary biological bondage. How she proposes to subjugate the moon the reader is not informed, but the subjugation of men becomes the focus of the novel.

Her first quarry is Isaac, who will later become the Wandering Jew. Salome is a mere adolescent when she first meets Isaac but their passion, once aroused, is destined to prove enduring. Centuries pass, and Salome wanders adventurously about the Middle East, at one time the wife to three successive kings of Arabia; at another the consort of Zenobia, queen of Palmyra, whom she persuades to reform her kingdom into a female-dominated society. Still later, she passes through Europe, finds Isaac again, in Egypt, and experiences a rekindling of her early passion for him. Nevertheless, the lovers choose to defer, for another century, the ripening of their love to its consummation. Salome wanders on. She becomes the inspiration and power behind the legendary Pope Joan, and the voices that lead and direct the even more famous Joan of Arc. In search of an ideal, feminist kingdom, she journeys later to the Russia of Catherine the Great, and the England of Victoria. Ever frustrated in her attempts to better the lot of her kind, she once again finds Isaac who finally believes that their love is ripe for marriage. Salome realizes in wedded bliss that all her drive for power had been nothing but frustrated love. She even condescends to conceive and give birth to a child whom she names Homuncula, little man. And so Salome, as all women should, falls into line.

The Wandering Jewess as champion of women's liberation had

been presented in a serious vein in a fin-de-siècle German drama, *Ahasvera* (1895), by Victor Hardung. Here Ahasvera wrestles with innumerable problems confronting women, and her cause seems justified by the gravity of the issues that make up the plot.

Near the turn of the century, in response to virulent manifestations of anti-Semitism, political Zionism was born. The Zionist idea, the ingathering of Jews from their Exile to Zion, began to penetrate into the consciousness of Jews, and some Gentiles. The First World Zionist Congress in 1897 made headlines. Not surprisingly, the Wandering Jew-Jewess theme, adapted to every other issue, served also as a vehicle for comment on Zionism. Hans von Kahlenberg's *Ahasvera* (1910) presents the Wandering Jewess as the mother of a young Jew who attempts to liberate world Jewry from Gentile oppression and lead them to Zion.

A great many modern issues found articulation through the medium of this myth. As a fallen angel like Quinet's Rachel, or a saintly maiden like Merville and Maillan's Esther, the Eternal Woman brought salvation to mankind. As an earth-mother like Sue's Herodias, she is the champion of the oppressed—the defender of the Huguenots in their struggle against the Jesuits. As a lusty seductress like Gutzkow's Salome, she is Everywoman transcending the social mores of her time and serving as an agent of satire on nineteenth-century literary society. As an ambitious amazon like Viereck and Eldridge's Salome, she becomes the mouthpiece of anti-feminists, while as Hardung's Ahasvera, she is a defender of women's rights, and, as Kahlenberg's Ahasvera, the mother of a Zionist prophet.

Ever since her creation, woman has been considered the complement of man, not an entity apart and independent. She has been understood solely in terms of her man—as wife, mother, sister, daughter, and lover—and seldom in terms of her own individuality. She is seen as a reflection of men's needs. No wonder that the Wandering Jewess, the myth of womanhood, also appears primarily in the role of wife, sister, daughter, mother and lover. No wonder that the Wandering Jewess, as Woman, is believed to be either salvation or perdition to men. She is either angel or demon—both measured by her performance toward men.

The Rabbinic interpretation of the Genesis term[6] denoting "helpmeet," the creature that was to be woman, discloses precisely these elements in her image. "If he (man) is worthy," say the Rabbis, "she is a help; if not—she is an opponent." Woman's sole purpose in creation is to serve man's needs; hence, even her character depends on man's virtue: if he is deserving, she will turn out good, if he is not, she will turn out bad. Angel or demon: for her man.

1

The Virgin-Madonna

> But it is not necessary to look into esoteric literature. From the Rebecca of *Ivanhoe* up to the Jewess of "Gilles," not forgetting the works of Ponson du Terrail, the Jewess has a well-defined function in even the most serious novels. . . . I think nothing more is needed to indicate the place the Jewess holds as a sexual symbol in folklore.[1]

The ideal woman is three women in one: she is mother, virgin, and temptress. No matter how absurd or paradoxical an amalgam of motherhood, virginity, and sexual allure may appear, this is the ideal of female perfection. Every man dreams of the perfect woman who combines maternal caring with erotic appeal yet retains a madonna-like virginal purity. Whether consciously aware of it or not, every man yearns for the succor of the womb, the challenge of seduction, and the security of virginal innocence.

This is the mystique of womanhood.

In early human history the basic elements of ideal womanhood were embodied in the figures of goddesses, worshipped as mystical mother images, that served both as objects and as mistresses of conquest. Clay figurines believed to be fertility idols have been unearthed by archaeologists in all parts of the globe. However, the celebrated goddesses of ancient mythology were representations of only one or another element of the ideal of femininity. Even the most sophisticated mythological system of antiquity produced but one-dimensional feminine deities: specialization was the key. Until the emergence of Christianity individual elements of feminine perfection were not incorporated into a unified theological idea.

It was Christianity that first brought all of these elements together seeing them in the person of Mary. No wonder Mary's appeal has been universal in Christendom. She has reigned supreme as the Virgin, Madonna, and Mother of Jesus; all roles informed by an aura of adoration not entirely free of sexual overtones.

Mary the Virgin has been venerated as Queen of Heaven, the ideal of sublime purity. Mary the Mother has been the subject of adulation as the consummate source of compassion, the maternal bosom offering solace and forgiveness. Mary the Madonna has been worshipped as the symbol of love.

No other woman in the history of civilization has been assigned such a comprehensive role. No deity has ever been conceived to encompass so completely all that men desired, ranging from the spiritual to the erotic. In all ages and from whatever angle her worship has been approached, the multifaceted image of Mary has not fallen short of the worshipper's expectations.

In secular literature this role has been assigned by Christian authors to the character of the Jewish woman. As if transposing the Mary figure from the realm of their religion to the realm of literature, the early creators of fiction fashioned the Jewish heroine out of the elements of the Mary image.

Why have Christian writers chosen the Jewess as representative of the feminine ideal of fiction? Why should devout followers of Mary pass over the Christian woman in their search for a literary heir to Mary? Why has the Jewish woman, rather than the Christian, been chosen as the symbol of Marian perfection in early modern literature, which was actually Christian literature? Was it because of the belief that the Jewish woman was a "racial" descendant of Mary, herself a Jewess? Have these Christians, students of the Bible, perceived the Jewish woman's implicit link with the Bible?

The Jewish woman, more than any other, evoked the bygone biblical era and the distant biblical milieu which bore and nurtured the Holy Woman of Nazareth. Christian authors saw in the contemporary European Jewess a product of the same environment, a carrier of the same traditions. Although sharing for centuries the lands and climes of her Christian counterparts, the Jewish woman was conceived as belonging to that faraway land of Judea, to that different air of Palestine. She was considered a direct descendant of Mary and the other ancient Jewesses who populated the pages of the Bible.

The biblical proto-Jewesses were in fact the first literary symbols of feminine perfection composed likewise of conflicting elements. Already in her debut in the Genesis account of Creation, woman appeared as the embodiment of a dual concept: she was both temptress and mother. And this startling dual image of womanhood persisted throughout the Bible.

She is called Hava, Eve, because she is to be "mother of all who live." Hava means *live* in Hebrew. But Woman, the potential mother of mankind, is first introduced in the role of temptress. Her flirtation with the snake and then her yielding to its temptation set the mood which reaches its climax when Woman seduces her man, Adam, and induces him to commit mankind's first sin. As if transfixed, man eats the forbidden fruit handed to him by Woman, and later admits he did so simply because "she gave it to me." No extreme coercion had to be exercised on her part. Unquestioningly the man follows the woman's lead. And the woman, with surprising facility, assumes the unprecedented role. This frivolous trifling with the fate of mankind is done by the same creature who later is endowed with the awesome power of reproduction—the first mother.

Women in the Bible acquire additional roles as the changing scene of the human condition requires additional capabilities. However, the established pattern of duality remains constant. Like a basic color scheme, it is manifest in each biblical heroine as she appears on the scene.

Each of the matriarchs has a particular allure. The stately image of Sarah, wife of Abraham, for instance, is not impaired by the legendary impact her beauty exercised on two ruling monarchs of her time. While to later generations Matriarch Sarah is the symbol of hearth and home, much is made in biblical commentary of her obvious physical charms and of the fact that not only did she arouse the passions of an Egyptian Pharaoh in her youth but duplicated this feat vis-à-vis the Philistine king Abimelech in her later years. The irresistible feminine appeal of this first mother of the Hebrew nation, the wise, prophetic matriarchal figure who dominates the early stage of history, caused consternation at the Philistine court.

Nor did the aforementioned monarch fare better with Sarah's daughter-in-law, the fabled Rebecca. This second Hebrew matriarch, the wife of Isaac and mother of Jacob and Esau, is depicted in the Bible as an enchanting woman. The couple's sojourn in Philistine Gerar during a famine in Canaan proved, because of Rebecca's beauty, perilous for both Isaac and the Philistines, whom God threatened to punish for their lustful intentions toward her. The encounters of Sarah and Rebecca with the court of the Philistine king, almost parallel incidents, were the initial sources of a clash between the two nations, later to become the classic adversaries of antiquity.

Tragic Rachel whose exquisite beauty overshadowed her contemporaries also embodies the duality of the female role. On one hand, she is the legendary "Mother of Israel." Her tomb on the crossroads near Bethlehem is a shrine where the destitute, the barren, the homeless worship. Jewish legend assures us that Rachel rises from her grave and weeps for her children driven into Exile. Jeremiah the Prophet consoles her with the promise of her sons' return to Zion. Thus, Rachel is inextricably interwoven with the exilic past and the redemptive future of the Jewish people. She is the nation's mother. Out of her flow sorrow, comfort, and hope. Her image as the mother of the Jewish nation is as alive today as it was two thousand years ago. It appears as a motif in art, literature, and music.

An even more popular image associated with Rachel is the romantic portrait of the striking beauty who is capable of commanding slavelike devotion: it was for her love that Jacob labored seven years. And seven more. As we shall see later it was this aspect of the Rachel figure which served as source material for a host of literary works by Christian writers.

Dinah, the only daughter of Jacob, was desired by the Canaanite prince Shehem to the extent that he committed the first recorded rape in history and plunged the Hebrews into their first act of war.

What about the other feminine figures of the Bible? Rahab of Jericho combined cunning and sexual appeal to earn her place in biblical history. And Yael the Kenite crowned Hebrew victory over the hostile Sidonites with a combination of feminine wiles, wisdom, and sheer spunk. The Sidonite Sisera never had a chance. While his army was defeated and dispersed by Deborah, the fiery Hebrew Prophetess-judge, he himself was lured into the tent and the deathly embrace of the young Kenite.

Ruth the Moabite is remembered not only for her selfless loyalty to Hebrew kin and country but also for her judicious use of Hebrew sexual mores to gain a husband in the tribe of Judah and establish the House of David.

Young King David drew Bathsheba into multiple sin. Years later though, Bathsheba the clever queen artfully maneuvered to secure the throne for Solomon, her son.

Young Abishag the Shunamite lives in collective memory as the nubile young woman whose warm flesh comforted the aging king, while Shulamite of the vineyard is remembered as the one who set Solomon, the young king, aflame. As the heroine of the Song of Songs, she is the romantic-erotic element of classical Hebrew poetry.

In Christian art and literature Shulamite is a mystical figure. In early Byzantine miniatures she symbolizes the Church in a dual image. She is either the bride of Jesus or the Virgin Mary. In a series of medieval interpretive illustrations to the Song of Songs called "Hortus Deliciarum," the Jewish maiden Shulamite is depicted as the Virgin flanked by monks on both sides while the daughters of Zion sprawl at her feet. The Church continued this extraordinary identification of Shulamite with the Virgin. For instance, in the sixteenth-century tapestry "Story of the Virgin" in Rheims Cathedral the identification is complete but with the roles reversed: it is Mary who is depicted as Shulamite. Medieval French and Spanish portraits of the Virgin with dark complexion, the celebrated "black madonnas," are in fact representations of the Shulamite described in the Song of Songs as "black but comely." Biblical metaphors for Shulamite, the "Rose of Sharon," the "Garden-dweller," and the "Fountain of the Gardens," were also interpreted by Christian theologians as references to the Virgin Mary. These interpretations must have provided the initial rationale for the association between the erotic Jewess of the vineyard and the Holy Virgin of the Church.[2]

Christian liturgical music also capitalized on the Shulamite theme in celebrations of the Virgin Madonna. English composers of the fifteenth and sixteenth centuries vied with their Dutch and Italian counterparts in providing musical background for verses from the Song of Songs. Some are delectable lyrics of love, others outpourings of passion singing the praises of both the Shulamite and the Madonna. Monteverdi's choral "Nigra sum" and "Pulchra es" were popular Marian hymns of the seventeenth century.[3] Cantatas, oratorios and symphonic poems picked up where liturgical music left off, and the phenomenon the Shulamite-Madonna entered Christian consciousness.

Christian exegesis did not however confine such association to the Shulamite. Another striking example is the identification of the Holy Virgin with Queen Esther, a most popular Jewish heroine. The central figure in a major episode of Jewish history, Esther was a young, beautiful Judean exile in Persia who enchanted the emperor and became his queen. When minister of state Haman plotted to annihilate the Jewish minority, Esther employed her tactical sense to turn disaster into victory. The tyrannical emperor, whose fierce temper had snuffed out the life of the previous queen, became a subservient subject of the fair Jewess. In his zeal to please her, he ordered the execution of Haman and the elevation of the Jew Mordechai in his place. A special scroll in the Hebrew scripture honors the role of Esther in Jewish history. It is read on Purim, a Jewish festival commemorating the event.

Medieval Christian iconography identifies Queen Esther with the Virgin Mary. Time and again Mary is depicted as the beautiful Jewish queen whose intercession with the Persian emperor on behalf of her people is interpreted as the Virgin's mediation with Jesus on behalf of mankind.[4]

A later Jewish heroine of even greater dramatic impact was Judith of Bethulia. The ultimate femme fatale, Judith of the Apocrypha occupies center stage in the Hanukkah story. When, during one of the Greco-Syrian campaigns against Judea, the resistance of her besieged city was about to crumble, Judith in a gesture of patriotic courage offered to save it. The young widow of devastating beauty managed to enter the enemy camp and secure an invitation to dine in the tent of Holofernes, commander in chief of the enemy forces. After dinner, as the influence of woman and wine lulled the mighty warrior into a stupor, Judith severed his head and brought it to her astounded people within the city gates. When his men discovered the disastrous after-effects of Holofernes' assignation with the mysterious Jewess, they fled in panic. Bethulia was saved, and the victory contributed to the eventual liberation of Judea from the Greeks.

This Jewish historical episode, perhaps more than any other, found fertile soil in literature and art. To an even greater extent than the relatively harmless Esther, deadly Judith has been a popular model for dramatists, painters, composers and sculptors of all times. Medieval Christianity's tribute is, however, the most flattering. Despite her violent option, despite the bloody nature of her act and the coldblooded aplomb with which she carried it out, Judith was deemed worthy of being identified with the Virgin Mary. In a daring gesture of justification, Judith's slaying of Holofernes was interpreted by the Church as the triumph of the Virgin over the Devil.

Both Esther and Judith are subjects of tapestries which hang in cathedrals, and of paintings by the greatest European masters like Donatello, Mantegna, Botticelli, Tintoretto, Giorgione, Veronese, Rubens, Cranach, Rembrandt, Poussin, and Michelangelo. (Judith is included in the Sistine ceiling.) Both are part of architectural designs in great churches. Their exploits are perpetuated in music by Doppler, Lefebvre, Honegger, Goosens, Handel and Milhaud. Both appear as central characters in drama and literature. The impact of these biblical heroines is inestimable.[5]

These two Jewesses were also exploited for political purposes. The Esther theme, for instance, served as an expression of public dissatisfaction with Henry VIII of England and his ministers in an anonymous verse play, entitled "A New Interlude of Godly Queen Hester," performed on the London stage in 1561. Huguenot playwright Antoine de Montchretien's "Esther," staged in 1585, served to champion the Huguenot cause under cover of biblical allegory. A century later, Madame de Maintenon, Louis XIV's formidable mistress, sponsored the great tragedy *Esther,* by Racine, to promote her own cause. In the play she was identified with Esther, the model of Christian virtues, while her rival, Madame de Montespan, the king's former mistress, was identified with Vashti, the personification of evil. The audience was fully aware of the allegorical intent, and the play, which has since entered the ranks of world classics, was an unqualified success.

As if to prove that Jewish women of later ages were indeed descendants of biblical heroines, the biblical female role pattern seems to continue beyond the biblical period. Perhaps Queen Salome Alexandra can be cited as the first post-biblical model. Her reign (1st century B.C.) is fondly remembered as a short but unique period of peace and prosperity in Judea's pre-Roman era. A Hasmonean princess, that is, a member of the Jewish royal dynasty which ruled Judea for about a century prior to the Roman conquest, Salome Alexandra was the wife first of King Aristobulus I, then, after his death, of his brother and successor, Alexander Yannai. She inherited the throne from Alexander and with it political and economic chaos. Within a short time, Alexandra, called "Shlomzion"—Peace of Zion—by her people, won the confidence of her subjects, rebuilt the state and strengthened its borders. She improved the economy, established domestic peace and international relations. Judea exercised great influence abroad through adventageous alliances negotiated by the queen. According to Rabbinic tradition, during Shlomzion Alexandra's reign the soil of Israel was so fertile that grain grew to extraordinary size—a sign of divine blessing.

The figure of another Hasmonean princess, the tragic Mariamne, is also a reincarnation of the biblical ideal. A great-granddaughter of Queen Salome Alexandra, Mariamne was the wife of Herod, the Idumean usurper of the Judean throne. His insane infatuation with the beautiful Judean princess and his subsequent jealous rage led to her own and her entire family's execution. Her victimization at Herod's hands enhanced her image of innocence and tragic beauty. It was undoubtedly the figure of Mariamne which introduced the element of tragedy into the Jewess image of literature.

The erotic-tragic Jewess image was reinforced by the figure of Berenice, the last Hasmonean princess of renown. Sister of Agrippa II, the last Jewish king to rule over Judea, the twice-divorced princess was the reigning beauty of Jerusalem. During the Roman siege of the city she made an unsuccessful attempt to mediate between the Jewish command and the enemy forces. When the Roman general Titus met Berenice, he fell passionately in love with her. Their love affair, which continued during the battle and final destruction of Jerusalem, scandalized the Jews. After the conquest of her country by her lover and his legions, Berenice followed him to Rome. There Titus established the Jewish princess in the royal palace and proceeded with plans to marry her. But Vespasian and the senate opposed Titus' marriage to the "beautiful barbarian." Finally, their twelve-year-long love affair ended with Berenice's banishment from Rome, caused perhaps by Vespasian's outrage at Titus' fits of jealousy, during one of which he had had a senator strangled on suspicion of flirting with Berenice.

Jean Racine's tragedy *Bérénice* appeared on the Paris stage in 1670, only one week before Pierre Corneille's *Tite et Bérénice* made its debut. The drama, the coincidence of the staging, and the success of Racine's production created a sensation which helped establish Berenice as one of the great dramatic figures of the theater. The London stage produced Thomas Otway's *Titus and Berenice* in 1676. A century later, Pietro Metastasio's popular *La clemenza di Tito* captured the Italian theater.

In the 5th century, almost a thousand years after the reign of Esther, Persian historical records mention a beautiful Jewish queen—her name is not preserved—who is first referred to as the wife of King Yezdegard I, and later as the queen-mother of his successor, Bahram V. At the same period, another Jewish woman, Hypatia, was prominent in Alexandrian Greek society. Long known for its tolerant cosmopolitanism, Alexandria began, in the late fourth century, to suffer from a sectarian Christian rule—anti-Greek, anti-heathen. As a Jew and a neoplatonist philosopher (her writings have not come down to us), Hypatia was associated precisely with those elements in the society most unacceptable to the Patriarch Cyril, under whom synagogues were converted into churches, Jewish communal and private property expropriated, and Jews stripped of their clothes. Humiliated and abused, the Jews were driven from the city in 415, the year, as well, of Hypatia's martyrdom.

Though the Prefect Orestes, Governor of Alexandria, sympathized with the Jews, he was powerless in the face of Cyril's atrocities which enjoyed the emperor's full support. Hypatia's fame as a brilliant philosopher and orator, in addition to her social prominence, singled her out for attention and, unfortunately, for a catastrophic fate. She became a tragic victim of mob violence, perpetrated by a group of fanatical Christian monks from the monastery of Mt. Nitra, near

Alexandria. Angered by Hypatia's skill in defending Judaism in countless theological debates and emboldened by the news of Christian riots in Alexandria, the monks seized the young Jewess and literally tear her to pieces. Hypatia thus earned the distinction of becoming the first martyr to Christian Jew-hatred.[6]

The list of Jewish martyrs to Christian fanaticism is long. With the advent of the Middle Ages and the rapidly declining fortunes of the Jews in Church-dominated Europe, the episodes of tragedy in which beautiful, brilliant Jewish women have had central roles multiply. These striking Jewish women have made an indelible impression on public memory—the stuff of which eventually fictional heroines were made. By the end of the Middle Ages when secular literature and drama were taking shape, the image of the fictional Jewess was well established. It had been fashioned out of various elements of historical memory. Central to those elements was the aspect of tragedy.

The rise of Islam created its own style of Jewish martyrdom and its own rank of Jewish heroines. Muhammad, the prophet and champion of Islam, encircled and then massacred most of the Jews of Arabia in the early years of the "jihad," the Muslim holy war against infidels. Among the trophies of his triumph, Muhammad collected three beautiful Jewish women and added them to his harem. One was Rihana of the Jewish Kuraiza tribe, the elite of Jewish Arab clans. The second was Safia, the widow of the tribal chief Kinana, himself murdered by Muhammad's men, when all the warriors of the powerful Khaibar tribe were lured into a trap under the guise of a peace agreement. The third, Zainab, was the sister of Marhab, a slain warrior of the same tribe.

Safia was Muhammad's favorite. Her name is even mentioned in the Koran. Zainab, a great beauty of fiery temper, refused to reconcile herself to the humiliation of being the wife of her people's dishonorable foe. She swore revenge. On one occasion when she was asked to serve the Prophet of Islam and several guests in his tent, Zainab poisoned their food. Muhammad survived but suffered from the effects of the poison for the rest of his days. Zainab was executed.

The surviving Jewish tribes were now prepared to fight Muhammad in open battle, rejecting his religious proselytizing and proposals of peace. Two young and beautiful Jewesses, poets of acclaim in the Arab world, were largely responsible for the defiant mood. Asma'a from among the Banu Khatama, whose elegant Arabic style won praise from Arab poets of the period, wrote biting satire about Muhammad's prophecies. Some of her poems were battle cries to her tribe to defy the "prophet of an inferior creed." Muhammad heard of Asma'a's poetry and was displeased by its popularity. He called for an avenger of his honor. One of his faithful volunteered to silence the spirited Jewess. The avenger crept into Asma'a's tent under cover of darkness and murdered her in her sleep.

The second Jewish woman to threaten Muhammad's conquest was the poet Sarah of Yathrib. In an elegy mourning the massacre of her people, the poet told how the leaders of fortified Yathrib (Medina), trusting the peace treaty, opened the city gates, and how then the Muslims with Muhammad at their head drew their swords and massacred men, women, and children in the Jewish city which had extended protection to Muhammad in his flight from his Arab enemies. The Prophet of Islam did not like the poem. Sarah, like Asma'a, was murdered by one of the Prophet's champions.[7]

The most formidable challenger of Islam among Jewish women was the Kahena. A Berber Jewess called Aures Damia, she was the Kahena (priestess) of a powerful North African tribe. In 687 she commanded the joint forces of several armies against the advancing Muslim troops of Hassan ibn al Nu'man el Ghassani. To the chagrin of the Muslims, the Kahena's armies fought them to a standstill. When a final victory drove the invaders from the area, the Kahena united under her rule the entire Maghreb (North Africa), a feat never before and never since accomplished. The Jewess Aures Damia became the queen of the Maghreb, bringing it peace and unprecedented prosperity until 702. In that year the Muslims renewed their onslaught on North Africa. This time, anticipating the superior tactical skills and indomitable leadership of the Kahena, they approached in overwhelming numbers. Fighting valiantly to the end, the Kahena was struck down by a Muslim sword. The North African front collapsed. With the Kahena's death no military leader was able to defy the invaders. One by one, the Berber armies surrendered to the Muslims, and the Maghreb passed under their rule unchallenged to our day.

The Kahena is a legend in North Africa. Her triumph, attained neither by Rome, the Vandals and Byzantium before her, nor by Muslims, Turks and Spain after her, colored the tales of glory surrounding her name. The unification of the Maghreb, although for no longer a period than fifteen years, was the unique achievement of a fierce, proud Jewess of biblical stature.[8]

In the eighth century when the legend of the Kahena was still a vivid historical memory, the Byzantine empire boasted a celebrated Jewish beauty as its queen. She was a Khazar princess. Her country, Khazaria, extending between the Volga, Dnieper and the Black Sea, was a powerful kingdom until the twelfth century when it fell to Slavonic tribes.

The Jewish Khazar princess was the wife of Byzantine Emperor Constantine V and the mother of his successor, Leo IV, called "Leo the Khazar," in reference to his maternal origins.

Another "Khazar lady of noble birth" figures among the heroines of Hungary's early history. Hungarian folklore has it that one of the conquering Magyar chieftains, a founding father of the Hungarian homeland in the Danube valley, was married to a beautiful Khazar princess. Byzantine chronicles substantiate the account, which served as basis for the controversial theory that Hungarian Jews are descendants of Khazars and thus blood-kin to Magyars rather than to Jews beyond Hungary's borders.

The obscure Khazar-Jewish-Hungarian princess brings us to tenth-century Europe. Now the focus of Jewish history shifts to the western regions of that strife-torn continent under Church domination. The Jews were the primary targets of a religious intolerance compounded by ignorance and superstitution. They were believed to be sons of Satan, accomplices of Judas, and killers of Christ.

The Church Fathers, in formulating the doctrine of deicide, pointed an accusing finger at the Jews; this provided a theological basis for anti-Jewish propaganda and the myths that reinforced it. Of all the accusations, the most devastating was that of blood libel or ritual murder—the myth that Jews killed Christian children in order to drain their blood for baking matzoh. In a sense, this myth reinforced the Christ-killer image of the Jew: killing Christian children was believed to be a periodic re-enactment of the killing of Christ. Every unexplained death of a Christian whipped the local populace into a frenzy of Jew-hatred, resulting in riots, show trials, public executions, massacres and burnings. From the first recorded blood libel case, that of William of Norwich in England, who was said to have been crucified by Jews during Passion Week in 1146, until the celebrated Beilis case in Russia in 1912, the blood libel claimed thousands of Jewish lives in different parts of Europe and resulted in loss of property and domicile for many more. Similar in force to this was another myth that made Jewish existence in Christian Europe untenable: the belief that Jews poisoned drinking wells and spread the plague among Christians.

Centuries of agitation by the Church culminated in wholesale devastation of Jewish communities by the various Crusades. They initiated an era of death and destruction that permanently changed Christian-Jewish relations. The ills released by misguided mob passions established precedents of abuse that could never again be recalled. The myths of the evil Jew—as killer of Christian children, poisoner of wells, blood-thirsty usurer and wandering bogey man—were born during the height of the Crusades when leading clerics exhorted the mob to "kill the enemies of Christ" at home, even before setting out for the Holy Land. Never again was the Jew secure in Europe.

Church Councils legislated the myths into permanent decrees, isolating the Jew more and more, forbidding him to associate with Christians, ordering him to wear a distinguishing badge, expelling him from certain areas, and finally incarcerating him in ghettoes. Worst of all, the anti-Jewish violence unleashed by the Crusades resulted in a distorted, negative image of the Jew. This image entered literature in the figure of the stereotyped Jew villain.

Paradoxically, the Jewish woman remained untouched by the anti-Semitic bias affecting the Jewish male. Although she was not spared the suffering meted out to her people—as a matter of fact, the Jewish woman was often singled out for martyrdom—her positive image remained intact. Despite hatreds and suspicions, the Jewish woman of literature, and of reality, remained the beautiful, brilliant ideal of womanhood from the Bible.

Out of these Dark Ages the first fascinating Jewess to emerge is Raquel of Toledo. The chronicles of Castile refer to her simply as "La judia hermosa," the beautiful Jewess who kept King Alfonso VIII enchanted for seven years—neglecting wife and kingdom—until her violent death at the hands of his jealous queen. Raquel was widely regarded as the mythical evil spirit of Spain, and her death as the deliverance of king and country. Her legend lived on in ballads, romances, and epic poems, which added colorful details to the romance and to the figure of the Jewess.[9]

Unfortunately Raquel had a twin in tragedy across the Pyrenees. Pulcinella of Blois (in the county of Chartres) is known for her poignant martyrdom. Count Theobald of Chartres became infatuated with this strikingly beautiful Jewish woman, and the countess, to intervene in the affair, initiated a rumor of blood libel implicating the Jews of Blois. The ruse worked: the local Jewish population was condemned to the flames by Theobald himself. Pulcinella alone was exempted by a special act of clemency. However, on the day of the public burning, 26 May 1171, Pulcinella defied the count and joined the Jewish community of fifty-one souls in martyrdom.[10]

A historical footnote draws an ironic parallel between the tragic episodes involving Raquel of Toledo and Pulcinella of Blois. Eleanor of Aquitaine, wife of Alfonso VIII of Castile who caused Raquel's murder was the sister of Alix, wife of Theobald who brought about

Pulcinella's death. They were the daughters of Eleanor of Guienne; Alix, by her first marriage to Louis VII of France and Eleanor, by her second marriage to Henry II of England.

The reign of Casimir the Great of Poland in the fourteenth century is considered the golden age in the history of the Jews in that country. Casimir extended the privileges his predecessor, Boleslav V, had granted the Jewish minority after settling them in Poland as merchants and supervisors on royal estates. Casimir succeeded in holding the restive clergy in check. The Jewish community flourished, establishing the first trade contacts with the West and bringing prosperity to Poland.

Some historians credit a young Jewish woman with the growing fortunes of Jews in Poland. She was "beautiful Esterka," the daughter of a poor Jewish tailor in Cracow. In 1356 the king installed her as his mistress in the royal palace of Lobzovo near Cracow, and during the course of years Esterka bore him two sons and two daughters. The sons were brought up as Christians and granted princely titles; the daughters were brought up as Jews.

After Casimir's death, Esterka and her daughters were banished from the royal castle by his successor, King Louis of Hungary, who also abrogated Jewish privileges. Poland's mood changed. In response to anti-Jewish agitation, a pogrom swept through the Jewish sector of Cracow: Esterka and both her daughters were massacred.[11]

With the increase of clerical power, episodes of Jewish martyrdom also increased. The tragic tale of "Golden Rose" is one of the most touching incidents of Jewish history. When in 1603 a group of Jesuits expropriated the synagogue of Lvov for a monastery, the Jews appealed to the royal court which granted their petition. The local archbishop, however, refused to comply with the royal order, and the Jews of Lvov despaired of ever having their house of prayer restored to them. Rose, the rabbi's wife, requested an audience with the archbishop in order to make a personal plea. When the prelate saw the beautiful woman, he was overcome by an emotion even more compelling than compassion. He agreed to restore the synagogue to the Jews of Lvov if Rose consented to become his mistress. But, he warned, if she refused, the Jews would be banished from the city.

Rose consented on condition that first she might deliver the permit with the seal of the archbishop to her people. When the beloved wife of their rabbi returned with the desired document, the Jews greeted her with jubilation. As they streamed into her house with prayers of spontaneous thanksgiving, Rose stole up to the roof and leaped to her death.

Another memorable martyr was Adel Kikinis, the daughter of a well-to-do merchant and the wife of a leading member of the Jewish community of Drohobicz. Adel was known as "the mother of the needy." Her reputation for humanity and charm had won her many admirers among the Christians of the town. Though the local clergy preached against her, Adel's popularity seemed unassailable.

On the eve of Passover, 1718, Adel's Christian maid was induced by clerics to conceal a child's corpse in the Kikinis' cellar. The next morning, when the dead child was "discovered" in the Jewish house by local police, the maid related that she had been forced to murder the Christian child on orders from her mistress and several members of the Jewish community, to obtain Christian blood for the Passover service. Adel and a great number of Jews were arrested. When prolonged torture yielded no confession, the entire group was threatened with execution. Adel Kikinis felt responsible for the distress of her fellow Jews and decided to save them by sacrificing herself. She told her interrogators that it was she who had carried out the ritual murder: all the others were innocent. The clergy eagerly accepted her testimony; the others were released, and Adel was condemned to burn at the stake. Upon hearing the news, however, her maid broke down and confessed the truth. The clerical court brought a new verdict: although innocent of the crime of ritual murder, Adel Kikinis was pronounced guilty of anti-Christian acts. Her sentence was reversed on condition that she submit to baptism. Adel's refusal to accept Christianity sealed her fate. She was executed in the public square of Drohobicz, on 17 September 1718.

> On the eve of the Sabbath, on the twenty-seventh day of the month of Elul in the year five thousand four hundred seventy-eight the saintly lady Mme Adel, daughter of Rabbi Moses Kikinis, was condemned, and she sanctified her soul for the sake of all Israel. May the Lord avenge her blood, and in this merit may her soul have everlasting life.[12]

The tombstone of Adel, which bears these words, became a Jewish shrine.

Did this travesty of human values which condemned the unfortunate Jewess to agonizing death shake the town she had showered with her generosity? Did the Christian poor who had benefited from her goodness cry shame at such an act of inhumanity? The reaction of witnesses is seldom recorded. We do know however that anti-Jewish agitation on the part of the clergy continued unabated, and that Jewish life in Poland and Russia sank ever deeper into the quagmire of hate and prejudice.

In Italy, a number of Jewish women rose to prominence through a classic combination of "Jewish" virtues—striking beauty and various talents. For example, the fame of Giustina Levy Perotti's grace and gift as orator-poet in fourteenth-century Venice was immortalized by Petrarch's verses in her honor.

In the seventeenth century, though the Inquisition threatened the world of learning, Jewish women occupied prominent places in art and scholarship. Already in early youth Sara Copia Sullam was renowned as a gifted musician. As she grew into womanhood she became an accomplished linguist, poet, and the dazzling hostess of a salon frequented by the highest Venetian society.

Ansaldo Ceba, the scion of a patrician Genovese family who had exchanged a brilliant diplomatic career for clerical robes, read Sara Copia's poetry and "fell in love with the generosity of her heart." He was later so moved by her beauty that he conceived "an intense yearning to be united with her soul." So he claimed in his love letters to Sara Copia, letters in which, to promote their union, he also used every means of persuasion to convert her to Christianity. Even when he fell fatally ill, from his deathbed he continued his desperate compaign of conversion. After his death, the letters of Ansaldo Ceba were published by one of his disciples, and the extraordinary love affair between the Jewess and the Catholic divine became public.

Baldassar Bonifaccio, the bishop of Capodistria, took great interest in the affair. The much publicized friendship and Father Ceba's premature death—for which Sara Copia's recalcitrance was blamed—prompted him to take action against her. Bishop Bonifaccio published a discourse which gave "proof positive" that she denied the immortality of the soul. The charge was a potential death sentence.

When the pamphlet appeared, Sara Copia's friends believed all was lost. She began to work on a refutation, in defense of her life. She worked desperately, and two days after the appearance of Bonifaccio's treatise, Sara Copia Sullam's manifesto of refutation was presented to the tribunal of the Inquisition. It was a remarkable document, an erudite and incisive essay demolishing every charge advanced against her by the Catholic divine. She was totally exonerated. Her brilliant exposition defeated the Catholic bishop before the harshest of Catholic tribunals, and saved her from the flames.

Her close brush with death and the wave of hostility released by the controversy broke the proud but sensitive woman. Soon after the incident Sara Copia Sullam died.[13]

In Spain and Portugal, ever since the Jews' expulsion at the end of the fifteenth century, only underground Jews called Marranos survived. But they, too, were victims of spectacular trials, public burnings, floggings and expulsions. For they were invariably members of the higher echelons of nobility and even clergy. Their arrest as secret Jews always made a great stir, and the resultant grisly punishment by fire made for fascinating diversion.

Surprising numbers of Marrano women were trained in the arts and sciences of the age and occupied positions of importance. Many were well versed in the classics and conversant in several languages. For instance, Isabella Enriques "was famous in the academies of Madrid for her talent" of poetry, according to Miguel de Barrios, who dedicated two poems to her in his "Aplauso metrico" (1673). Isabella was a poet of such distinction that the Spanish literary community in Amsterdam elected her as member of Belmonte's Academia de los Sitibundos. Another, Isabella de Correa, was "as celebrated for her beauty as for her wit."[14] She was elected to the membership of the Spanish Academy in Amsterdam. A sizable number of Marranos left Spain and Portugal for a haven in the Netherlands where they openly professed Judaism. Among de Correa's admirers was Nicholas de Oliver y Fullana, the Majorcan author and cartographer who, in order to marry her, converted to Judaism.

The beautiful Marrano woman played a significant role in literary image making. Her spectacular black hair and white skin, large dark eyes and "oriental" features became the standard for Jewish beauty. In literature and on the stage, this was the image of the biblical heroine reincarnated. This was the Virgin-Madonna in contemporary form.

The first such Jewess to appear on the stage, Abigail in Christopher Marlowe's *Jew of Malta* (1589), was undoubtedly modelled upon a young Marrano woman who was brought to London through a remarkable incident a year before the staging of the play. She was seventeen-year-old Maria Nuñez Pereyra who together with a shipload of Marranos was fleeing from the Portuguese Inquisition to Holland. The boat was intercepted by an English vessel commanded by a cousin of Queen Elizabeth who fell in love with the strikingly beautiful Maria. When his ardent suit was spurned, the English captain diverted the Marrano ship to England and imprisoned its passengers in a London jail.

The news of the incident created a sensation in the English capital. Even Queen Elizabeth's curiosity was aroused by rumors of the young woman's great beauty and, according to contemporary accounts, she took her on a ride in her carriage through the streets of London. The queen then persuaded the infatuated captain to release his captives and guaranteed them safe passage to Amsterdam.

Maria Nuñez's name appears in the town records of Amsterdam for November 1593. It is in the marriage record of a twenty-three-year-old woman to another former Marrano after the couple's re-conversion to Judaism.[15]

Even the mystery and passion plays, the earliest literary-dramatic expressions of popular Christianity, portraying the life and death of Jesus, though notorious in their vilification of the Jew, presented the Jewish woman in a glorified light. The female characters in these religious plays were representations of the pious women of Jerusalem and Galilee, mentors and followers of Jesus, who wept at his passion and were first to witness his resurrection. "Indeed," remarks Chateaubriand, "the Jewish women did not participate in the humiliation and torture of Christ. They showed compassion to him. Therefore Jewish women were spared the malediction heaped upon Israel. . . ."[16]

The Jewish woman was spared Christian malediction only in literature and the arts. During the Reformation when religious drama and art reverted to Old Testament narrative for subject matter, biblical heroines served as symbols of Christian virtues. As we have seen, Shulamite, Esther, Judith, Rachel and Rebecca were major characters in allegorical plays and artistic representations. These biblical beauties were fifteenth-century style box office hits before being transposed into secular literature. Marlowe, Shakespeare, Lope de Vega, and Racine plucked the idealized biblical heroine from the religious drama of an earlier age, and transplanted her into a secular medium without regard for contemporary reality.

What was contemporary Jewish reality in the sixteenth and seventeenth centuries? What was the Jewess's reality? In Venice the first ghetto walls were built, followed by others in Frankfurt, Prague, Worms, Berlin, Vienna, and Budapest. Church Councils regularly imposed new taxes and disabilities upon the Jews, shut them out of the guilds, and forbade social intercourse with Christians. The Jewish woman, alienated from Gentile society, struggling with poverty imposed upon her family by the harsh rule of the Church and lord, intimidated by Christian hostility, was a frightened young girl, a harassed housewife or a careworn mother. Her husband or father, the itinerant peddler of used clothes and useless trinkets, was an object of ridicule set upon by zealous, misguided rabble, and often failed to return with the meager pickings of his trade. Then the Jewess joined the ranks of orphans and young widows the Jewish quarter boasted in overwhelming numbers. Her father or husband was no usurer skimming the fat off the poor Gentile. That, too, was a myth. By the sixteenth century money-lending had long been preempted throughout Europe by Italian bankers.

While in reality she was incarcerated in the ghetto living in fear of physical abuse, while her clothes were marked by a badge of shame, and the Christian midwife was forbidden to help deliver her babies even in an emergency, the Jewess in literature and on the stage reigned as an adored sex goddess, the young, carefree, pampered daughter of a rich Jew.

It was in the literature of England, France, and Spain—all of which at this time had no Jewish populations—that the most spectacularly glamorous Jewesses appeared. Perhaps it is not surprising that this should be so. The culture having the least contact with Jews would be the most prone to unrealistic portrayals. Having only sporadic contact with Jewesses in the flesh, the shapers of fiction were unhampered by reality in their image making; they were free to rely on sources like the Bible or an occasional celebrity for the most idealized image of the Jewess, the Virgin-Madonna of all ages.

2

Victim of Ritual Murder

Who's this? Fair Abigail the rich Jew's daughter
Become a nun! Her father's sudden fall
Has humbled her and brought her down to this:
Tut, she were fitter for a tale of love
Than to be tired out with orisons:
And better would she far become a bed,
Embracèd in a friendly lover's arms,
Than rise at midnight to a solemn mass.[1]

Abigail of Christopher Marlowe became the prototype of the "beautiful Jewess," the perfect all-purpose instrument. Her virtues served the needs of the times, and the particular framework within which the Jew was to be vilified. The fabulous Jewess was magnetic and lovely, innocent and beguiling, according to the style of the period, but she was always a sex object and almost always tragic. Although the details of plot might vary with the period, its basic features were constant. It was a pre-packaged story complete with an idealized image, a semi-orphaned state (she is brought up without a mother), a high-born Christian lover, and of course the wicked, old, rich Jew as father.

He is immutable, "the rich Jew." A symbol of evil in Christian literature, he is immortal. The ultimate evil: he is the killer of Christ and Christian children. He became rich from robbing poor Christians, and is eager to boast about how, with his "extorting, cozening, forfeiting"

> And tricks belonging unto brokery,
> I filled the jails with bankrupts in a year,
> And with young orphans planted hospitals. . . .[2]

Barabas, Marlowe's Jewish villain, in his time surpassed even Shylock in popularity. He did not step into a historical vacuum. Although three hundred years had passed since the last boatload of Jews left the shores of England, driven out by hatred and prejudice, Jewish presence persisted there. The Jew as bogey man lived on in folktales and ballads, in chronicles, religious plays, and songs. When Cromwell in 1615 proposed that the Jews be readmitted to England in order to improve its commerce, William Prynne voiced his opposition on the "solid proof" of historical memory, explaining that the Jews of England "had crucified three or four children at least, which were the principal causes of their banishment." And when in the nineteenth century Charles Lamb, the English critic, was asked how he felt about Jews, he answered: "I should not care to be in habits of familiar intercourse with that nation. I confess I have not the nerves to enter their synagogues. Old prejudices cling about me. I cannot shake off the story of Hugh of Lincoln."[3]

The story of Hugh of Lincoln. A sad piece of evidence of the mind's capacity to project guilt upon another. In 1255, eight years after Innocent IV issued a papal bull condemning the myth of ritual murder, the Jews of Lincoln were accused of crucifying an eight-year-old boy named Hugh. A contemporary chronicler, Matthew of Paris, describes all the supposed elements of the story, the torture and bloodletting, the crown of thorns, the mockery—a re-enactment of Jesus' crucifixion—and the all too real outcome: the cruel forms of execution of "the richer and higher order of the Jews of the city of Lincoln."[4]

Despite papal protests, the blood libel lived on. In 1279 some Jews of London were torn to pieces because of a similar accusation. In 1283 in Mainz, in 1285 in Munich, in 1286 in Oberwesel, in 1482 in Rinn, in 1491 in La Guardia . . . and in Blois, Vienna, Saslav, Zhytomir, Prague, Trent . . . in Budweis, Bern, Paris. . . . Was there an area free of victimization? Mass hysteria reached beyond the Middle Ages and turned Jewish reality into darkness and death, and Europe into an arena of anguish for the Jew—a proto-Auschwitz.

England remembered the "Jewish crimes." The bizarre accusations of ritual crimes were never proven, not a single trial yielded any evidence other than mass malice. Yet the myth penetrated the collective memory forever.

Members of the intelligentsia, statesmen, thinkers, and artists contributed to the myth making. Among them, the masters of literature bear a major share of responsibility. Marlowe's Jew villain is mob hysteria distilled into an artistic medium, presented on the legitimate stage. Marlowe's Jew villain, from the forum of the London stage, convinced Elizabethan audiences and the rest of educated Europe that the killer Jew—the outsider—was still alive; that he was more sinister than ever and that his hatred of Christ still knew no bounds. He would stop at nothing; his Christ-killer instinct drove him to murder even his own child.

Audiences flocked to the theater and saw the Jew villain plan revenge against all Christians, and cold-bloodedly kill his own daughter when she became a nun. They saw the Jew carry out ritual murder on his own child because she dedicated her life to Christ.

Barabas is a usurer ensconced in a mansion shared with his only daughter and some rascally servants who help him in his machinations against Christians. Fair Abigail is innocent of her father's hatred and of the evil which motivates him. Her love for the young Christian gentleman, Don Mathias, is full of trusting devotion and a naive confidence in a happy outcome. Don Mathias's love for the Jewess is likewise directed toward marriage.

Barabas has other plans. The wealthiest merchant in Malta, he refuses to surrender half of his riches to the governor and is stripped of all possessions as penalty. He swears revenge. Determined to regain his wealth and avenge himself on the Christian ruler, he chooses his daughter as the instrument of his evil scheme.

Although he claims to love Abigail dearly ("I have no charge, nor many children but one sole daughter, whom I hold as dear as Agamemnon did his Iphigen: And all I have is hers.")[5] he uses her with unmatched brutality. First, he persuades her to pose as a repentant Jewess wishing to convert to Christianity and become a nun. With this deceit she is to appear before the abbess of the nunnery now located in the Jew's expropriated mansion. Once initiated into the order, Abigail is secretly to remove a box of gold and jewels hidden under the planks of the bedroom floor, and smuggle it out of the house. The loving, loyal daughter consents to do her father's bidding. She accomplishes the devious mission and recovers for the villain the means to renew his campaign against the Christian governor, and against Christianity in general.

Abigail is employed as the agent of deceit a second time. When Lodowick, the governor's son, hears from Don Mathias of Abigail's great beauty, he decides to visit her in her house under the pretext of buying a diamond from Barabas. The cunning villain is delighted with the visit. As a helpless fly into the web of a spider, the unsuspecting young Christian innocently wanders into the trap of the scheming old Jew. Pretending to be too busy to receive him, Barabas instructs Abigail to "entertain Lodowick the governor's son with all the courtesy you can afford; provided that you keep your maidenhead."[6]

Against her will and amid protestations of love for Don Mathias, Abigail obeys her father and receives Lodowick with charming manners and smiles, entrapping him into promises of betrothal. Having obtained this, Barabas secretly incites Don Mathias into challenging Lodowick to a duel. Playing into the hands of the Jew, the two young Christian nobles fight each other to the death. The grief of the governor, of Mathias's widowed mother, and of his own daughter is a source of joy to this demon who draws justification for his deeds from his Jewish faith: "These are the blessings promised to the Jews, / And herein was old Abram's happiness: / What more may Heaven do for earthly man / Than thus to pour out plenty in their laps. . . . / Rather had I a Jew be hated thus, / Than pitied in a Christian poverty: / For I can see no fruits in all their faith."[7] "It's no sin to deceive a Christian; / For they themselves hold it a principle, Faith is not to be held with heretics; / But all are heretics that are not Jews."[8]

When Abigail discovers that her lover was the victim of her father's devious scheme, her grief turns to shock and despair:

> Hard-hearted father, unkind Barabas!
> Was this the pursuit of thy policy!
> To make me show them favor severally
> That by my favor they should both be slain?
> Admit thou lov'dst not Lodowick for his sire,
> Yet Don Mathias ne'er offended thee:
> But thou wert set upon extreme revenge,
> Because the governor dispossessed thee once,
> And could'st not 'venge it, but upon his son
> Nor on his son, but by Mathias' means;
> Nor on Mathias, but by murdering me.
> But I perceive there is no love on earth,
> Pity in Jews, or piety in Turks.[9]

She decides to renounce all earthly pleasures, and become a nun. The only hope of salvation, she believes, is in Christianity. The Jewess, as woman, opts for love through the only available avenue open to her: she enters a nunnery in order to devote her life to the religion of her lover.

The avenue of love within the Jewess-Christian stereotypical pattern leads to inevitable doom. Abigail is not permitted by literary convention to find solace in her sacrifice. In a blind rage after discovering his daughter's act, Barabas conspires to poison the food of the pious nuns. He sends a donation of cooked rice laced with venom to the depository of the nunnery. The nuns, Abigail among them, die a slow, agonizing death. Dying, Abigail bears witness to her love of father and Christianity in one. With her last breath she enlists the aid of a friar to save her father's soul through the grace of baptism. Confessing her share in the murder of Lodowick and Don Mathias, she pleads for secrecy on the part of the monk so that her father should not be charged with the murder:

> To work my peace, this I confess to thee;
> Reveal it not, for then my father dies.
> ... Death seizeth on my heart: ah gentle friar,
> Convert my father that he may be saved,
> And witness that I die a Christian.[10]

This dying affirmation of Christianity is underscored with irony: to the holy friar, her death is, more than anything else, the loss of a sex object. The friar responds to her words, "I die a Christian":

> "Ay, and a virgin too; that grieves me most."[11]

The tragic destiny of the Jewess can hardly be presented more poignantly. The banality and the utter futility of her great sacrifice are perfectly summed up in the cruel casualness of the friar's remark. Even after her initiation as a nun, Abigail remained the stereotyped Jewess.

Under the impact of anti-clerical trends in eighteenth-century France and Germany, attitudes towards Jews began to undergo a dramatic change. Voices calling for Equality, Liberty, and Brotherhood prepared the mood for the French Revolution and a new dawn for European Jewry. Ghetto walls began to crumble in several places in Germany and the first Jewish hero—Lessing's "Nathan the Wise"—appeared on the German stage.

Enthusiasm flared. The Jew was extolled in idealized terms as unrealistic as those that had been used to vilify him. Passionate voices called for admitting the Jew into the ranks of humanity, for granting him equal citizenship. The momentum carried some leading philosopher-politicians to the point of claiming that the Jew was capable of patriotism on a par with Christians, that he could learn to become a useful member of society. It was a heady mood, this rash optimism which ushered in the Age of Reason, and closed the doors on the Middle Ages in Jewish history.

The new trend was threatening to some Christians. To rehabilitate the Jew meant to deny his guilt, to deny the divine edict which ordained that he live in a state of abject misery as long as he continued to reject Christianity. Some believed that the status quo of Jewish oppression had to continue in order to validate Christianity's claim that the Jew's suffering served as testimony to his rejection of Christ. In order to maintain the status quo of Jewish oppression, popular hatred of the Jew had to be maintained.

The vision of the Jew as Christ-killer was revitalized by fresh references to ritual murder. Pope Benedict XIV called attention to a fifteenth-century ritual murder myth, the story of Blessed Andrew of Rinn (1482), by granting in 1754 plenary indulgence to all who went on pilgrimage to the church at Rinn where the relics were honored. This was followed in 1755 by the bull Beatus Andreas, the official beatification of the child martyr with clear reference to Jewish ritual murder although "there was no charge, no trial, no condemnation," writes bbé a Vacandard in his critical study of religious history.[12]

The motif of the Jew as ritual murderer served a similar purpose in Spain, where there had been no Jews since their expulsion in 1492. Their negative image had to be revived from time to time in order to keep the popular hatred alive. For this reason an anonymous child, allegedly martyred in La Guardia in 1491, was raised to sainthood in 1785. The parish priest of La Guardia confirmed the saintly status of the child by writing in that year that "it was universally believed that God had completed the parallel between Christ and the Niño, and on the third day had carried the body up to heaven."[13]

This child martyr, known only as the "Holy Niño of La Guardia," had no name—perhaps because there had never been a body to use as evidence against the Jews. Yet on 16 November 1491, five Jews, three of them "conversos," had been arrested by the Inquisition, strangled, then burnt; two more were torn to pieces by red-hot pincers.[14]

In 1789, four years after the sainthood of the Holy Niño was confirmed, novelist Gustavo Adolfo Becquer's popular novel *La Rosa de Passion* reminded Spaniards of the horror of Jewish ritual murder through the shocking story of Sara Levi's martyrdom at the hands of her father. Playwright Vicente Garcia de la Huerta in the drama *La Raquel* (1778) had adapted the Raquel-Alfonso theme to include a Barabas-like Jewish villain who as surrogate father slays the Jewish heroine. Both works, by reinforcing the institutionalized rumor of ritual murder, helped establish it in the public's mind as factual. Although "not a single case has ever been historically established," writes Abbé Vacandard, the rumor persisted even into the Age of Reason. Repetition was the only proof. Repetition in tales and chronicles, in plays and novels, created its own truth. And the fabulous Jewess as victim was a memorable and effective means of substantiating the myth.

Sara Levi, the saintly Jewess in Becquer's *La Rosa de Passion,* is Abigail in a Spanish eighteenth-century milieu. Product of a despicable Jewish household, she yearns for salvation through Christianity. Her yearning for the "true faith" gradually alienates her from her Jewish environment and finally lands her on the secret path to baptism. The unfortunate convert is in dread of her fanatic father and his friends. Soon her fear turns into a premonition of doom. When Daniel Levi finds out that his daughter has secretly converted to Christianity, he conspires with members of the Jewish community to lure the unsuspecting girl at night to a secluded spot near the Jewish cemetery; in a ghastly ritual presided over by the father they murder her, then dispose of the body without a trace. However, a miracle occurs: a rose sprouts on the spot of her martyrdom. The miraculous passion flower is the only witness to the gruesome blood sacrifice by Jews.

De la Huerta's Ruben became the most celebrated Jew villain of Spanish drama. A combination of English and German models, he is ruthless yet cowardly, sinister yet comic. The advisor of Raquel, Queen of Castile, Ruben exerts an evil influence on her and continually plots to secure favors for himself and his coreligionists to the detriment of Christians. Like Barabas, he uses the beautiful Jewess as his means of wreaking havoc on Christians, and then proves to be an instrument of her doom. When his evil deeds incite the populace to an uprising against the Jewish queen, instead of defending his daughter-surrogate, he cowers in fear behind the throne.

Raquel, on the other hand, does not panic; she does not hide. She faces her enemies with a serenity born of her love for Alfonso, the king. Her fearlessness and pride paralyze the would-be assassins. They hesitate. In a gesture of defiance she proffers her chest to their swords and challenges them to slay her. As they waver, the leader of the conspiracy discovers the Jew Ruben behind the throne. He thrusts the sword into the Jew's hand, and orders him to kill the queen. As the sharp steel penetrates her chest, Raquel cries out in pain—in anguish of betrayal, of victimization, of parting from her great love. Ruben, like Barabas, must also die for his crime. The victimizer is also a victim.

Both Daniel and Ruben are evil Jewish fathers within the framework of the Barabas-Abigail pattern: both murder lovely daughters devoted to Christians. Sara, the victim of Daniel Levi, is devoted to Christianity as a whole; Raquel, the victim of Ruben, is devoted to one Christian. Daniel Levi is the classic Christ-killer: he is motivated by hatred of Christianity. Ruben is a dishonorable creature in an age of chivalry: he is motivated by cowardice and self-interest. Both are "typical" Jews.

When the momentum of eighteenth-century tolerance carried positive attitudes towards Jews also to England and held out to them the promise of equal rights, some writers hastened to remind the public of "typical Jews" in the form of the classic Jew villain. Among these only Bulwer-Lytton employed the device of the ritual murderer.

Bulwer-Lytton's Almamen in the novel *Leila* (1838) reenacts the bloody deed more than two hundred and fifty years after Barabas. Leila, like Abigail and Sara Levi, is a delicate Jewess whose exquisite beauty and goodness make her into an ideal victim of ritual murder at the hand of a wicked Jew. Again like Abigail, Leila flees to the bosom of Christianity in despair over hopeless love for a non-Jew. At the solemn moment when the young Jewess, standing in front of the baptismal font, with a sense of exaltation intones her vows to her new faith, Almamen appears, brandishing a dagger. To the horror of all the assembled, the old Jew thrusts the dagger into the heart of his terrified young daughter and flees from the church. Leila, the tragic victim of avenging Judaism, collapses in the arms of her lover, Muzza the Moor, who arrives in time to witness her tragic destiny but too late to save her from it.

Bulwer-Lytton's close adherence to the Marlovian pattern is remarkable in light of a major difference in the story. Here the non-Jewish lover is a Moslem, not a Christian. Yet the disconsolate Jewess, in rejecting Judaism which prevented her romance, converts not to Islam, the religion of her lover, but Christianity. Bulwer-Lytton's Jewess is the most affirmative witness to the truth of Christianity. Unlike all other Jewesses whose primary objective in choosing Christianity was to be reunited in faith with their lovers, Leila chose Christianity despite the fact that it was not the faith of her lover. The author's message is clear: even in an age of secularism, Christianity remains the only road to salvation. The Jewess, in ceasing to reject Christ, becomes the target and eventually the victim of the Christ-killer Jew.

In Russia, where the presence of Jews in large numbers was a relatively recent phenomenon, the myth of ritual murder also arrived relatively late. At the end of the eighteenth century when, through annexation of eastern Poland, Russia inherited about a million Jews, it also inherited not only the "Jewish threat" but its panacea as well: anti-Jewish myths to curb Jewish prosperity and influence, anti-Jewish myths to keep the Jews in a state of misery.

It was not long before Lermontov, the nineteenth-century Russian poet and disciple of English masters, imported a Jew villain—the only sinister, truly frightening Jew to appear in Russian literature. Later there was no need for sinister Jew villains. The Jew ceased to be a threat in Russia. Victimized, decimated, brutalized by isolation and poverty, the Russian Jew by the middle of the nineteenth century was a harmless entity.

Lermontov borrowed the Abigail-Barabas theme in toto for his poem, "Whither So Swiftly, Young Jewess?" The "young Jewess," Sara, has a secret affair with a young Christian, but her old, sinister father finds out. He lurks in the shadows, spying on the young lovers. While the beautiful Jewess hastens to a secret meeting, the poet warns of the doom awaiting her. In the style of young love, she ignores obvious dangers. She flouts the taboo of Christian-Jewess union and rushes into the arms of her beloved. No sooner do the two meet than the arm of the old Jew reaches out, knife in hand. In a flash, Jewess and Christian collapse lifeless to the ground.

Here, in a deviation from the pattern, the daughter is not the only ritual sacrifice. The Christian shares with the Jewess the role of victim.

Lermontov's portrayal of the Jew as capable of a defiant act like murder is unique in Russian literature, where commonly the Jew is depicted as a timid clown, a ludicrous rascal incapable of an act which presupposes courage. There are no other Russian Jew villains reminiscent of Barabas or Almamen. Russian literary Jews are primarily contemptible foils to the beautiful Jewish heroine, their stature too insignificant to qualify for true villainy. They are stupid cheats and cowardly liars providing comic relief rather than inspiring fear.

English literature remained supreme in this respect. Marlowe's Barabas, Shakespeare's Shylock, Bulwer-Lytton's Almamen and Dickens's Fagin are quite incomparable in their villainy. Jew villains of other cultures never quite measure up.

German literature did not produce a true Jewish killer until the Nazi era. The traditional Jew of German literature was similar to the Russian model. Both were far cries from Barabas, the embodiment of all the Jew myths, the prototype of Jew villains. To Barabas, evil is not incidental but, as he boasts, it is the prime objective of the Jew:

> As for myself, I walk abroad o' nights
> And kill sick people groaning under walls:
> Sometimes I go about and poison wells;
> And now and then, to cherish Christian thieves,
> I am content to lose some of my crowns,
> That I may, walking in my gallery,
> See 'em go pinioned along by my door.
> Being young, I studied physic, and began
> To practice first upon the Italian;
> There I enriched the priests with burials,
> And always kept the sextons' arms in ure
> With digging graves and ringing dead men's knells:
> And after that I was an engineer;
> And in the wars 'twixt France and Germany,
> Under pretence of helping Charles the Fifth,
> Slew friend and enemy with my stratagems.
> Then after that I was an usurer...
> And every moon made some or other mad,
> And now and then one hang himself for grief,
> Pinning upon his breast a long great scroll
> How I with interest tormented him.
> But mark how I am blest for plaguing them....[15]

But the Jew is not permitted to have the last laugh: ensnared in his own trap, his wicked soul is extinguished in a cauldron of boiling water. Christianity is triumphant. The Jew, no matter how formidable a foe, is crushed in the end. His death is a just retribution for the ultimate crime of ritual murder—a fictional rationale for all the mass murders perpetrated against Jews on the pretense of their having committed that ultimate crime.

Lovely Abigail, Sara Levi, Raquel, Leila—pious, innocent young Jewesses committed to Christianity and sacrificed on the altar of Judaism—serve as reminders of the ritual crime. Time and geography are irrelevant. The only relevance is the common denominator of their symbolic role in a propaganda campaign which spanned several centuries and a variety of cultures. Becquer's martyred Sara Levi, for instance, was still a popular figure in post-World War II Spain. A version of her tale was performed as a choral recital on the Madrid stage in 1955.

The medieval myth of ritual murder as anti-Jewish device was most effectively kept alive in the version that had a beautiful Jewess as victim. The scenario of a father killing his own daughter, especially if she is the darling of Christian audiences, is especially horrifying. Is it any wonder that the ritual murder myth was as alive in Cromwell's

England as it had been in the Middle Ages, and that it served as an excuse in William Prynne's argument for the Jews' continued banishment?

The Jewess in all these works became her father's victim because of her devotion to Christianity. How much more plausible, how much more credible, was the murder of a Christian child by the same Jew. Modern secular drama and literature thus picked up where medieval myth left off. As victim of ritual murder the Jewess bore visible witness not only to the truth of Christianity but, just as importantly, to the corruption of Judaism and its murderous intent. The Jewess of these works served to reinforce the idea the Church formulated early in its history: the Jew is redeemable only through baptism. No other avenue should be open.

3

Struggle for Emancipation

But she is so good
So lovable!
A dreamer none the less.[1]

The good, lovable dreamer is Recha, daughter of Nathan the Wise, the product of a new era. It is the Enlightenment of the eighteenth century which provides an alternative for the Jew. Its anti-clerical, secular mood seems to open a gate for the Jew, an avenue of acceptance other than baptism.

Recha is the daughter of the first Jewish hero of literature. Gotthold Efraim Lessing, the humanist, philosopher, and playwright, in defiance of literary convention's holy cow, the Jew villain, put a Jewish hero on the German stage. It was a bold move. In the face of popular tradition, Lessing's Jew was a shining example of humanist values: tolerance, wisdom, and love of mankind. Modelled after Lessing's admired Jewish friend, the philosopher Moses Mendelssohn, Nathan is the positive reproduction of Shylock: he is noble where Shylock is knavish, he is loving where Shylock is hating, wise where Shylock is foolish, and caring about others where Shylock is criminally egocentric. Nathan is as unrealistically superhuman as Shylock is subhuman.

The prominence of Lessing helped make Nathan into the prototype of the fictional Jew hero almost to the same extent as Shakespeare's popularity established Shylock as universal Jew villain. Within a relatively short span of time Nathan bred multi-cultural imitations: in literature and on the stage, in German, French, English, and Russian, Nathan-type Jewish heroes began to appear.

Not that the Jew villain was displaced by this new arrival. On the contrary, every heroic Jew seems to have bred several villainous Jews in novels and in the theatre. But a precedent was set. An impression was made. A first important step in the struggle for Jewish civil rights had been taken. Even though it took a hundred years after the appearance of Nathan the Wise on the Berlin stage in 1779 for Jews in Europe to be fully emancipated, the first breach was made in the seemingly impregnable wall of anti-Jewish public opinion.

To set the record straight, the first good Jew in drama was Tobias Smollet's "honest Hebrew" in *The Adventures of Count Fathom* (1753). But Smollet's Jew, the kindly money-lender Joshua Manasseh, was a minor character in the play and did not exercise an appreciable impact. Lessing's Nathan, however, was the central figure in a drama named after him. The fact that Lessing's play became very popular also helped turn Nathan into a revolutionary phenomenon. Nathan became a larger-than-life symbol of Enlightenment, a dramatic display of the period's glorified expectations. Smollet's Manasseh, although likewise unrealistically benign and generous (he refuses to take interest on money advanced to poor Christians), never reaches Nathan's heroic stature. He is a "typical Jew" with repulsive looks and an unpleasant voice reminiscent of the familiar Jew villain. Nathan, on the other hand, is handsome, dignified, elegant, and well-educated, very much the perfect gentleman of the Enlightenment.

It is significant that Smollet's Manasseh, the first Jew hero of English letters, made his appearance in the year when the first "Jew Bill," a bill granting naturalization to all British Jews, was introduced in Parliament. The uproar in the chamber, when the measure came before the Commons for discussion, was echoed throughout the country. Sermons, speeches, pamphlets noisily debated the issue. Anti-Jewish agitation reached such a fever pitch that within months after its passage in the summer of 1753, the bill was repealed "as a point of political policy." Subsequent years saw the controversy continue as the issue of the Jews' civil rights generated a lively interest in all spheres of English life. In literature, the Jew as wicked money-lender dominated. Fanny Burney, Samuel Richardson, Henry Fielding, Charles Macklin and Samuel Foot vied with one another in presenting despicable Jews on the stage and in the novel, swelling the tide of opposition to Jewish civil equality.[2]

Tobias Smollet's positive Jew was paralleled by a "kindly" reference, in one of Oliver Goldsmith's *Essays* (1758–1765), to a "Mr. Jacob Henriquez, who, though of the Hebrew nation, hath exhibited a shining example of Christian fortitude and perseverance."[3]

Attributing "Christian" virtues to Jews was the kindest gesture a Christian could make toward this people who had been accused of an absence of virtue for centuries. The battle for Jewish emancipation was fought by Christians and Jews alike utilizing this argument exclusively: time and again pro-Jewish speakers and writers attempted to prove the Jews' "Christianness," in addition to their usefulness to Christians.

Lessing, of course, concentrated on the Jew's qualities as a true son of the era. "Christian" virtues were now, for a brief period, identified as "humanistic." And so, in his drama, the Jew is a "humanist."

Lessing retained aspects of the pattern established by Marlowe and Shakespeare. The mature Jew has a young daughter, a good and lovable and very charming maiden who at the outset falls in love with a very heroic and handsome young Christian. But there the similarity ends. Tension mounts as the audience expects the familiar drama to unfold, from the ecstasy of forbidden love to the agony of the Jewess-Christian dilemma, culminating in tragedy. But the plot takes an unexpected turn. Recha (Rachel), the Jewess, who at the beginning of the play is saved from fire by the "angelic" Templar (the scene is set in Palestine during the Crusades) and begins to dote on him, turns out to be not a Jewess at all. She is a foundling, abandoned at birth by Christians and Moslems alike. The Jew, a member of the much-maligned minority, had taken pity on the child and embraced her with love and kindness. As upon his own daughter, he has showered the best of his world upon her, generously imparting knowledge, ethical teaching, and material gifts.

Recha has grown up to be a proud specimen of Enlightenment virtues, a genteel girl and a devoted daughter. Nathan has spared her the pain and travail of the world, and now wishes to spare her the pain of rejection by the Christian Templar who spurns her when he discovers that she is a Jewess. At the risk of losing a loving daughter, and even his own life, Nathan decides to disclose Recha's Christian parentage. But before he has a chance to do so, he finds out the Templar's family name, and a vague suspicion prompts him to keep silent. Instead, Nathan's otherwise loyal Christian maid reveals the secret to the Templar. In anger the Christian knight hints at Nathan's guilt to the Jew-hating Patriarch of a local monastery who promptly prepares for the Jew's arrest and subsequent burning at the stake—the punishment for having educated a Christian child in the Jewish faith.

Saladin, the Moslem ruler of Palestine, suspects the Templar to be his long-lost brother and befriends him in order to examine the striking resemblance at closer range. At the same time Saladin has occasion to make Nathan's acquaintance and, despite his prejudices, is so impressed by the Jew's extraordinary character that he swears friendship to him. He dissuades the Templar from proceeding against the Jew. Meanwhile Nathan finds out that, because of the Patriarch's denunciation, he is in mortal danger. His only concern however is for the happiness of Recha and the Templar. His careful investigation reveals that the Templar and Recha are brother and sister, children of Saladin's lost brother. At the climax of the play, when Nathan discloses this in front of all concerned, the general rejoicing creates an aura of goodwill toward the Jew. The dramatic conclusion was expected to promote goodwill beyond the footlights towards Jews in everyday dealings and attitudes.

The changing emotional climate of the age brought about a change of heart also among English authors. Quite a few who had earlier presented the blackest of Jew villains now included heroic Jewish characters in their writings. Smollet himself, the creator of the first English Jew hero, had five years previously portrayed one of the most deplorable Jew figures in *The Adventures of Roderock Random* (1748). Similarly, Sheridan's good Jew in *The School for Scandal* (1777) was preceded by a wicked Jew in *The Duenna* (1775). Richard Cumberland's greedy, unscrupulous Jew in *The Fashionable Lover* (1772) was followed, twenty-two years later, by the central figure in *The Jew* (1794), a noble, kind-hearted money-lender, "the widow's friend, the orphan's father, the poor man's protector." The Jew as universal philanthropist, like the wise Nathan of Lessing.

All Jewish heroes of this period have a common denominator: their chief virtue lies in their usefulness to Christians. The kindly money-lender lends to poor Christians without interest. The honest peddlers sell below cost. Other Jew heroes save Christian lives at the risk of their own, deliver goods amid perilous circumstances, and frequently convert to Christianity out of love. The most popular service rendered by heroic Jews, however, is the adoption of abandoned Christian children.

These abandoned Christian children brought up by the good Jew are exclusively girls. The ingredients of the plot which eventually became a pattern are unvarying. The kindly Jew embraces the Christian infant rejected by her Christian kith and kin and brings her up as his own. The young Christian receives a Jewish name and a Jewish education, Jewish love and indulgence, and grows into a beautiful

Jewess like all other beautiful and desirable Jewesses of Christian literature. Her true identity is known only to the wise and loving foster father. The Christian lover inevitably appears and inevitably falls in love with the maiden he believes to be an irresistible Jewess. At the dramatic moment when her happiness with the Christian hangs in the balance, the self-sacrificing, devoted Jew reveals the secret of her true birth. With one gesture he brings happiness and bliss to a number of Christians. The marriage between the two young people can take place, the parents of the groom are spared embarrassment, and the Christian Church regains a soul.

It is interesting that the prototypical plot of Lessing was modified in this fashion. For Lessing's Jew did not bring Recha up in the Jewish faith—faith is not mentioned in her education—nor did he return her to the Church. Furthermore, the Christian lover turns out to be not a Christian and not a lover: both sister and brother are Moslems. Lessing's humanistic objectives created these anti-stereotypes, both in characters and in the incidents of the plot.

The imitations are Christian-centered. Although not unkind to the Jewish image, plot and characters tend to be self-serving and patronizing rather than genuinely emancipatory. In German literature, Johann K. Lotich presents the Jew Wolf in *Wer war wohl mehr Jude* (1783) as the adoptive father of Marie, a Christian waif returned to the Church; and in Karl Steinberg's *Menschen und Menschensituationen* (1787), the kindly Isaac Mendel rears Recha's namesake for eventual Christianity. In Kotzebue's *Kind der Liebe* (1791), the compassionate Jew comes to the aid of a Christian woman bearing a "child of love" who, in her hour of dire need, is heartlessly abandoned by members of her own family and faith. The Jew Isaac, in Hensler's *udenmädchen n von Prag* (1792), offers to pay the bill of a poor Christian neighbor whose plight is ignored by his other neighbors, though they are fellow Christians.

While Lessing's lead in literature initiated a growing change in attitudes toward Jews, assisting in their struggle for civil rights, the voices of opposition also changed. The Jew villain of German literature, an admixture of rascally cheat and ludicrous clown, now acquired a new dimension. With the threat of increasing Jewish power, the contemptible little "Mauschel" figure lost some of its validity. Anti-Jewish writers found it expedient to introduce a new element of fear into the ingredients of their portrayal, an element of evil mystery reminiscent of the medieval Jew figure.

Early evidence of this regressive trend appeared in France. At the same time that Lessing was writing in order to effect a change in age-old attitudes against Jews, Jacques Cazotte wrote his novella *Rachel, ou la belle juive* (1778) in order to reinforce them. In Cazotte's story, the element of "black" magic in Rachel's feminine charms is reinterpreted and posed as the central issue of the plot. Here Rachel's bewitching potential as Woman becomes black magic and the Jewess herself becomes an instrument of evil. Cazotte, a Jew-hating member of a religious society, believed that French political life was riddled with charlatans practicing black magic. Through the figure of Rachel he chose to implicate the Jews.

In Cazotte's tale, Ruben is an evil magician in possession of a magic mirror. When King Alphonse mockingly commands him to conjure up the most beautiful woman in Spain, the face of Rachel materializes in the mirror. He is overcome by her extraordinary beauty, and orders Ruben to bring Rachel to the palace at once. She comes, and the king's infatuation increases, reinforced by a spell placed upon a small portrait of Rachel which Alphonse wears at all times. In order to free their sovereign from the evil, the king's men conspire to kill the beautiful Jewess while Alphonse is on a hunt. Strangely, when Rachel is stabbed, the king on a distant hunting ground falls unconscious from his horse. In order to revive him, his trusted aide opens his shirt, rips Rachel's picture off his chest and flings it into the mud. A recuperated Alphonse returns to Toledo, heartily approves of Rachel's murder, and orders the Jews banished from the kingdom. The evil spell lifted, peace returns to the tormented country.

The implications of this theme are abundantly clear. Cazotte's was one more voice that, during the Enlightenment period, was added to those of some *philosophes* who, though glorifying reason, relied on age-old prejudice and ignorance in their opinions about Jews. They believed the Jews to be a backward, obscurantist people, vestiges of a barbaric past. Even Voltaire and Diderot reiterated medieval stereotypes of the Jew villain, insisting that hatred and superstition were basic to the Jewish personality.

A theme similar to Cazotte's appears in the work of Johann Christian Brandes who introduced to German literature the figure of the frightening Jew in possession of evil magic powers. In his play, *Rahel oder die schöne Jüdinn* (1789), the charming, innocent Jewess, the Christian loving foil to the Jew villain, is now *"die reizende Zäuberinn"* —"the enchanting sorceress." Not only is she an accomplice in the crime but a main source of evil power. Rahel is the German equivalent of Cazotte's Rachel, in a less passive role. No longer the mere instrument of evil magic, Rahel is a willing participant in corruption and the manipulation of power for the benefit of

Jews and the detriment of Christians. Her death, likewise, is not a cause for grief but celebration: it is the logical conclusion to a life of corruption.

Conrad Gottlieb Pfeffel, in his poem "Alfons und Rahel" (1799), echoes both the theme and its treatment. The Jew and Jewess have demonic dimensions, in the service of some distant supernatural evil authority, forerunners of the pre-Nazi Jew myth.

The change of approach to the Jewess figure is of special interest to us. Although otherwise a rare occurrence, the negative Jewess figure is endemic to this period. What accounted for it?

During the last decade of the eighteenth century several Jewish women achieved glittering social prominence as hostesses of cultural "salons" in Berlin and Vienna, and later in Paris and London. The most celebrated among them was Rahel Levin, in whose popular salon the upper classes of German society mingled with writers, poets, and composers. Prince Louis Ferdinand, Prince Radziwill, Baron Alexander von Humboldt, Friedrich Schlegel, Clemens Brentano and Friedrich Schleiermacher were frequent visitors. Goethe was introduced to German society in her salon and so were the compositions of Mozart. Rahel married Karl August Varnhagen von Ense, a Prussian diplomat, converted to Protestantism, and became Antonia Frederika, shedding even the name that had tied her to Judaism.

Rahel Levin had met the Prussian aristocrat in the salon of Henrietta Herz, a beautiful intelligent Jewess, whose soirées attracted conservative blue-bloods and young liberals alike, including Count Mirabeau, Schiller, Rückert, Niebühr and Jean Paul Richter. Emperor Frederick William of Prussia granted a pension to the Jewish woman in her old age in recognition of her patriotic contributions to German civic life.

The other famous Jewish socialite to meet her Prussian husband-to-be at the Herz salon was Dorothea Mendelssohn Veit, the daughter of Moses Mendelssohn and wife of banker Simon Veit. Because of her wealth and intelligence, her salon was likewise a meeting place for intellectuals, politicians, and men of high finance. Dorothea, the mother of four, scandalized Berlin society by leaving her husband for the young Romantic writer and philosopher, Friedrich Schlegel. In her search for identity, Dorothea Mendelssohn converted to Protestantism, and later to Catholicism, after which the Catholic church solemnized her union with Schlegel. They settled in Vienna where their home rapidly became a gathering place for the elite of Viennese society. Her novel *Florentin* (1801) was hailed by some critics as an outstanding literary work of the era. She also translated Madame de Staël's novel *Corinne* (1807).

Fanny Arnstein, a charming, talented Jewish woman of celebrated taste held court in the social-cultural world of Vienna. Among her admirers was the Emperor Joseph II. A count of Lichtenstein was killed in a duel for her sake. She was the co-founder of the Music Society of Austria which made Mozart's career possible.

In London the Rothschild women dazzled British society. Hannah Cohen Rothschild was courted by many eligible bachelors of British aristocracy before her marriage to Nathan Rothschild. Charlotte, wife of Hannah's son Lionel, the first Jew to receive a British title (the first Baron Rothschild), was hostess to prime ministers, foreign diplomats and literati. Her frequent guests included the heir apparent, Edward VII, an ardent admirer of beautiful Charlotte. Hannah's granddaughter became Lady Jane Roseberry, wife of Philip Primrose who was Britain's foreign minister for over forty years and its prime minister from 1894 to 1895. Queen Victoria in the company of Prime Minister Gladstone attended her funeral and recited the prayer for the dead. Jane's cousins, Annie and Constance Rothschild, also married members of British nobility. Darlings of the British social set, they cruised with Kaiser Wilhelm II, dined with Lord Balfour, and paid visits to Queen Mary and her daughters.

Baroness Betty de Rothschild presided over a celebrated social salon in Paris where Rossini, Meyerbeer, Heine, Balzac, Orsini and Napoleon III were frequent guests.

Though these, and other charming, talented Jewish women were winning respected positions in society, the vast majority of Jews were still living in ghettoes struggling with civil disabilities which included humiliating body taxes, loyalty oaths, restrictions on livelihood and residence. The coveted emancipation was still mostly a mirage hovering on a distant horizon. The spectacular social success of these socialits or *Milieujüdinnen* was no indication of Jewish conditions. It indicated only the financial accomplishments of a few Jews, and the glorification of their "fabulous Jewesses," real-life exemplars of the fictional Jewess image.

The token Jewish darlings of high society were a source of fear and resentment to some. Men like Cazotte, Brandes and Pfeffel refused to allow the medieval view of the Jew to disappear under the impact of Lessing's dramatic debate or Christian Wilhelm von Dohm's argument for the amelioration of Jewish conditions. They conjured up that image in the form of the evil magician just as the Nazi propagandists did in the form of the evil "defiler of Aryan purity" almost a century and a half later. In the mental world of Cazotte, and more so in that of Brandes and Pfeffel, Jewish women also played a role now as sources of fear. Rahel Levin was a figure of power on the social scene. It is probably not coincidental that the negative Jewess of literature is called Rahel, and is a woman in a high social position.

In Germany no real progress was made in the Jews' emancipation until the second half of the nineteenth century, although the first articulated suggestions for reform emanated from Germany. Dohm's pamphlet, *On the Civil Amelioration of Jews* (1781), stirred stormy debates in Germany and France, where it stimulated an essay competition by the Société Royale des Arts et Sciences on the question, "Are there ways of making the Jews of France happier and more useful?" Abbé Henri Gregoire's eloquent response won the prize and exercised an impact on attitudes toward Jews.[4]

The general climate of opinion was changing. In 1789 the Declaration of the Rights of Man, which implied Jewish equality, prepared the ground for the Revolution which in turn abolished all civil inequality. In 1791 France granted all its Jews citizenship, only the second country to do so, the first having been the United States, in 1776.

The struggle was long and vehement. Novelist Cazotte was not alone in his fierce opposition. He was a member of a group whose avowed aim was not only to prevent granting civil rights to Jews but to advocate their banishment from France, as, in his novella, the Jews and their evil spell are banished from Spain.

Cazotte and his friends wished to turn back the clock of history to fourteenth-century France, when the Jews were expelled and recalled four times until their final banishment in 1395. Jews began to settle again in Paris only in the eighteenth century but had no privileges whatsoever until the liberalist ferment began to draw attention to their plight. The first tangible result was the abolition in 1784, by Louis XVI, of the humiliating "body tax" paid per capita for Jews and cattle. When Napoleon Bonaparte extended recognition to Jews, anti-Jewish agitation flared up anew. The practical application of the Jews' citizenship rights was still a subject of heated public debate. Restrictions on business, residence, and legal transactions continued until 1846 when, more than half a century after the grant of citizenship, they were abolished by the Supreme Court of Appeals.

The fortunes of the Jewish civil rights struggle in France suffered greatly from the appearance on the Paris stage of a flagrantly damning character such as P. E. Chevalier's Rachel in *Rachel, ou la belle juive,* in 1803. Chevalier's villainous Rachel is the fruit of his hostility to Jews and of his agitation against their liberties in the post-Revolutionary period. Rachel was expected to be an Esther, destined to save her people, but turned out to be a Jezebel bringing ruin to Castile. His Rachel is a symbol of pride and ambition, and she is justly subject to punishment.

Napoleon's victorious armies carried the ideals of the French Revolution to the rest of Europe. Under their pressure, Jews were granted citizenship between 1808 and 1812 in all occupied German states. But the fall of Napoleon and the victory of the Holy Alliance spelt victory for reaction: conservatism and anti-Semitism were the dominant mood of the Congress of Vienna (1814–1815). All civil rights measures to Jews were repealed by the assembled heads of state from England, Prussia, Austria, France, and Russia. By day they fashioned statutes abrogating Jewish rights and by night they danced in the ballrooms of Jewish hostesses.

But the Jews of Europe continued their economic and social advancement despite their limited political status. During the course of the nineteenth century they moved into larger cities, entered industry, commerce, and banking. Some became rich; others, well-educated. Liberal professions opened to them. They were active in the cultural, scientific, literary, and art worlds of their countries. They were becoming a dynamic presence.

Jewish women became increasingly visible to the Gentile world. No longer was the Jewess image nourished solely by the intermittent appearance of individual Jewesses in highly romanticized roles. No longer was it a sensational event, as it had been in 1690 when Jewish singer Brentgen Marcus was invited to sing at the court of the Great Elector, for a Jewish woman to make her mark in the field of entertainment, literature, or art. An abundance of Jewish female talent burst onto the stages of Europe, establishing reputations that added new dimensions to the Jewess image.

Besides the fabulous trio—Rachel, Sarah Bernhardt and Ada Isaacs Menken, discussed in Chapter Five—there were numerous other Jewish stars. In the German theater Karoline Stern, in Italy Rahel, in Austrian music halls Sofia Wertheimer, in America Carrie Goldsticker, in the French opera Mlle. Bloch, in Hungarian and Austrian opera Karoline Bettelheim, Clotilda Kleeberg, Sophia Kaskel, Flora Friedenthal, Pauline Lucca, Louise Heyman, Margaret Herr, Charlotte Wolter, Josephine Wessely, Fortune Tedeschi, Rosa Csillag, the sisters Eichberg, Sulzer and Ries, Giuditta Pasta, Mina Wetzler—the list of acclaimed Jewish performers was truly impressive.

In England, the emancipation of Catholics in 1829 exercised an impact on Jewish fortunes. The following year a bill was introduced in the Parliament for the abolition of a discriminatory oath. Although defeated, the Parliamentary measure, which underwent three more readings in subsequent years until its passage in 1835, created renewed public interest in the Jews. The positive views expressed during these debates propelled the Jewish cause on a slow and tentative but definite course towards success. In 1871 the Jews of England became full citizens of their country—one year after their coreligionists in Germany, one hundred years after those in France.

English belle lettres greatly contributed to the controversy surrounding the Jews. Thomas Wade presented a "good Jew" in his play *The Jew of Arragon* [sic], or *The Hebrew Queen* (1830), with the express intention of aiding the cause of his "fellow residents of Jewish faith to gain full citizenship rights." He dedicated the play "To the Jews of England," and declared in the introduction: "I wish to add my weak and unknown voice to that gathering and all-prevailing power of opinion, which assents to and enforces your demand to be freed from those chains of exclusion with which you have so long, and so unjustly, been fettered by your country men." In order to achieve this, the author insists that "the main object of my work has been to embody, in a dramatic form, the struggles, the triumphs and sorrows of a noble Hebrew and his daughter amid the woes and oppressions of their mighty race."

In the play, another version of the Raquel story, Wade presents Xavier, a highly idealized Jewish father, and his fair, kindly, lovable daughter, Rachel. At the opening of the play, the striking Jewess appears at the side of her handsome, rich, elegant, and generous father bearing an enormous tribute to the king of Castile. The Catholic monarch falls in love with her, and soon thereafter makes her his queen, and the Queen of Aragon. The Jewish queen proves to be a blessing for all Aragonians, Christians and Jews alike. The aristocracy, however, resent her benevolent rule which enriches the common folk and strips the elite of power and wealth. On the occasion of the king's absence from the capital, they foment an uprising against her. As the riotous rabble approaches Rachel's quarters demanding her death, the gentle Jewess quietly swallows a vial of poison to end her life, a life dedicated to love of humanity.

In the same year that Wade's good Jew attempted from the boards of Covent Garden to sway public opinion in England, Walter Scott presented the dubious Jew figure Isaac of York in *Ivanhoe,* and eight years later Charles Dickens delighted readers and damned the Jews with the figure of Fagin in *Oliver Twist* (1838). Lord Macaulay made an eloquent plea in Parliament for removal of Jewish disabilities and his famous essay on the *Civil Disabilities of Jews* appeared in the

Edinburgh Review at the same time as William Hazlitt's vigorous defense of Jewish emancipation was published in *The Tatler* (1830). Dickens drew wide criticism for Fagin. In defense of his choice of the Jewish arch-thief as character, Dickens claimed that Fagin's Jewishness was incidental, and had no bearing on his attitude toward Jews.

Nevertheless, it was not until twenty-six years later that the great romanticist presented a Jew as hero, in *Our Mutual Friend* (1865). Mr. Riah, a benevolent, generous money-lender, thus joined the glittering ranks of one-dimensional super-Jews with virtues exaggerated to the point of absurdity. Mr. Riah never made it as an authentic Jew as did the robust, lifelike Fagin.

Two decades earlier, Maria Edgeworth was confronted with a similar dilemma. In the preface to *Harrington* (1817), the author's father, Lovell Edgeworth, reveals that the novel was written in response to an American Jewish lady's protest against the novelist's misrepresentations of the Jewish character. The letter of complaint by Miss Rachel Mordecai of Richmond, Virginia, prompted Maria Edgeworth to examine her motives in selecting Jews as villains. She realized that her Jewish villains were not the fruit of her own anti-Semitic attitudes but rather imitations of traditional literary types. In the first chapter of *Harrington,* through one of her favorite characters, she explains:

> . . . not only in the old story books, where the Jews are as sure to be wicked as the bad fairies, or bad genii, or allegorical personifications of the devil, and the vices in the old emblems, mysteries, moralities, etc., but in almost every work of fiction, I found them—invariably represented as beings of a mean, avaricious, unprincipled, treacherous character. . . .[5]

Harrington, a drastic reversal of her practice, became more than an atonement for her past sins: it was an eager attempt to undo stereotypes. In her effort to compensate, as so often happens, she overcompensated. Her good Jews are caricatures of goodness. They seem just as non-human as her bad Jews had been. To nineteenth-century readers, however, perfect goodness had just as much credibility as perfect evil, and the virtuous Jews of her last novel accomplished possibly as much good in the form of positive attitudes toward Jews as her earlier evil Jews had in the form of Jew-hatred.

The good Jew in *Harrington* appears in the foster-father role. He is Mr. Montenero, a superb gentleman merchant. To all appearances he brings up the charming Berenice as a Jewess and places at her disposal wealth and culture. Miss Montenero displays all the "typical" characteristics of a Jewess in looks and in personality. Harrington, the Christian gentleman who falls in love with her, does so because she is "different." He is attracted to that specific charm, that combination of "gentility" and sexiness only a Jewess of culture possesses:

> The dignified simplicity, the graceful modesty of her appearance, so unlike the fashionable forwardness or the fashionable bashfulness, or any of the various airs of affectation, which I had seen in Lady Ann Mowbray and her class of young ladies, charmed me perhaps the more from contrast and from the novelty of the charm. There was a timid sensibility in her countenance when I spoke to her, which joined to the feminine reserve of her whole manner, the tone of her voice, and the propriety and elegance of the very little she said, pleased me inexpressibly.
>
> Here was a woman who could fill my whole soul; who could at once touch my heart and my imagination. I felt inspired with new life—I had now a great object, a strong and lively interest in existence.[6]

The young Christian is befriended by Mr. Montenero and the other elegant, cultured, intelligent members of his circle. He is delighted in his association with Jews and enchanted with the delightful Berenice. But his family is less delighted, and much less enchanted. Clouds gather on the bright sunny horizon of the romance. A storm breaks loose when Mr. Harrington makes his intentions of marrying Berenice known to his family. His father swears to disown him. His mother takes seriously ill. Terrible moments of unbearable tension pass between the lovers. Mr. Harrington's agony is overwhelming: he is incapable of offending his family and abrogating his "duty" by marrying a Jewess. At the dramatic climax, Mr. Montenero announces that Berenice is in fact a Christian, "an English Protestant!"

> "I have the pleasure to tell you, Mr. Harrington that your love and duty are not at variance—Berenice is not a Jewess."
>
> "Not a Jewess!" cried my father, starting from his seat: "Not a Jewess! Not a Jewess!—give you joy, Harrington, my boy!—Give me joy, my dear Mrs. Harrington—give me joy, excellent—(*Jew*, he was on the point of saying) excellent Mr. Montenero; but is she not your daughter?"
>
> "She is, I hope and believe, my daughter," said Mr. Montenero, smiling: "but her mother was a Christian; and according to my promise to Mrs. Montenero, Berenice has been bred in her faith—a Christian—a Protestant."
>
> "A Christian! A Protestant!" repeated my father.
>
> "An English Protestant: her mother was the daughter of . . ."
>
> "An English Protestant!" interrupted my father, "English! English! Do you hear *that*, Mrs. Harrington?"

"Thank heaven! I do hear it, my dear," said my mother.[7]

The story ends on an ecstatic note. The solution to the dilemma is satisfactory to both Christian and Jewish readers, although the latter may perhaps feel a twinge of regret at losing such a lovely Jewess. But then they have a consolation: the very fact that the fabulous heroine was so universally admired is to their credit. Even though a Christian, Berenice's virtues are those of a typical Jewess. Environment rather than heredity accounted for them. Her upbringing by a Jewish father produced a fitting wife for an upper-class English gentleman. No more eloquent voice was needed to convince the English public of the Jews' social acceptability.

While her physical beauty is frequently alluded to it is never described. We do not know how Berenice Montenero looked, except that she struck the protagonist at first sight as unusual and a "Jewess!" He caught a glimpse of her in the crowded theatre and, without knowing her, he knew her "race." The author, however, makes sure to emphasize her virtues, and they make her into a paragon of contemporary social values:

> There were, besides, in her manner and countenance indications of perfect sweetness of temper, a sort of feminine gentleness and softness which art cannot feign nor affectation counterfeit; a gentleness which, while it is the charm of feminine manners, is perfectly consistent with true spirit, and with the higher or the stronger qualities of the mind.[8]

Berenice Montenero is of course very much like Rebecca of York in *Ivanhoe* and the beautiful Jewess of Anna Maria Porter in *The Village of Mariendorpt* (1821). This novel, appearing also during the upsurge of pro-Jewish sentiment, portrays the very accomplished, high-principled Jewess as the perfection of feminine capabilities:

> Nature had given this young woman a mind as extraordinary as her person. Strong sense coupled with so much stronger feeling that upon all emergencies she rarely acted prudently—yet never unwisely—marked her character: strength far beyond her sex, yet united with so much beauty of countenance and figure, distinguished her appearance. Whenever her impassioned heart led her to adopt a wild scheme for attaining some coveted object, her powerful intelligence enabled her to conduct it ably: and the capacity of her body for enduring every species of fatigue, privation and change of weather, made enterprises within her reach, which would have been impossible for another woman.[9]

Woman power is epitomized through the figure of the Jewess. Porter, like several writers after her, sought to address herself both to the injustice done to Jews and the injustice done to women through the same fictional figure. With her novel she anticipated the first Suffragette Society founded in 1853 in her country. *The Village of Mariendorpt* supplied the basis of Sheridan Knowles's play, *The Maid of Mariendorpt,* produced in 1838.

Why is the foster-child role confined to girls exclusively? The objective of portraying the Jew in the best possible light, that is, in a role which benefits Christian society most, could have been as well achieved with a boy as foster-child. However, this would present some obvious difficulties. Since the ultimate aim in the complex story line is the Christian's return to Christianity, with a boy this would be more difficult: the physical signs of ritual Jewishness are indelible! Also, a girl was considered more likely to integrate into the Christian faith through the love of a man. A boy educated in Jewish culture and traditions would be less likely to abandon Judaism even for the love of a Christian woman. A boy's Jewish education was much more extensive, and Christian writers expected it to exert a more lasting influence. Finally, it is the woman who, in the true romantic tradition, follows her man, even to the extent of severing ties of family and faith. Also in true romantic tradition, the woman adhered to the feminine ideal—seductiveness masked as sweet submission.

The foster-child pattern is placed in a fresh context by George Eliot in *Daniel Deronda* (1876). Here it is a boy who is the subject of concealed religious identity, and that identity is Jewish, not Christian. The climactic revelation and return to faith refers to Judaism not Christianity. The solution to the Christian-Jewess dilemma lies in the Christian's change and not its reverse: it is the man who follows the woman. Once again, feminist and pro-Jewish arguments coincide.

In *Daniel Deronda* there is a first genuine effort at emancipating the Jewish character. In all other works of the age dedicated to the improvement of the Jews' social and political status, the Jewish heroes are unrealistically idealized; they are merely attractive vessels for beautiful ideals. Eliot's Jews are permitted the luxury of having values of their own. Although they, too, possess glorified personalities, they are not employed solely in serving the Christian world that would otherwise reject them. George Eliot allows her Jews to utilize their virtues for the betterment of their own people.

Ironically, the Jews of Germany received their coveted citizenship rights simultaneously with a rapid deterioration of attitudes towards them. In 1870, the newly established German Reich incorporated

Jewish civil rights into its constitution. But the new Germany became the bastion of conservative reaction, anti-liberalism, and narrow-minded patriotism. The Jews identified with the ideals of the German nation: their loyalty and patriotic fervor were unsurpassed by any German. Their valor had been tested in two wars for the German fatherland, and they distinguished themselves in numbers and bravery. During the Napoleonic wars (1813–14) they had fought for Germany against Napoleon with heroic devotion, despite their awareness of Napoleon's role in Jewish emancipation. A Jewish woman, Louise Grafemus (born Esther Manuel), received the Iron Cross for her extreme heroism. As sergeant of a Prussian cavalry regiment she led her men to victory despite her heavy injuries. In the Franco-Prussian War of 1870–71, out of six thousand Jews on the battlefield, four hundred and fifty-eight were killed, three hundred and twenty-seven received the Iron Cross.

The victory of Prussia over France, and the emergence of the Reich as a direct result of that victory, plunged the German people into a feast of national self-glorification. The Jews had no place in it: they were aliens. The ghost of their Christ-killer image was still haunting them when another manifestation of the Jew myth, the Jew as threat to German identity, surfaced in literature, and threatened their newly-won freedom. Anti-Semitic pamphlets, pronouncements, political parties, and slogans proliferated. The foreboding climate of political reaction concealed less and less the approaching dark clouds of the twentieth century.

German poet Günther Walling, in his attempt to counter the rising voices of political anti-Semitism in his country, returned to the Raquel theme. In his poem "Rahel von Toledo," written in 1887, Rahel is a beautiful Jewess caught in a massacre in the ghetto of her native Toledo. Fleeing in terror from the murderous Christian mob, she feels her strength waning. A mounted knight approaches. Not recognizing the king, she throws herself to the ground and begs him to protect her and her fellow Jews. Although bruised and clad in bloody rags, the exotic beauty captures the king's heart. Brandishing his sword, he scatters the mob and takes Rahel to his palace where he changes her rags for "purple velvet and silk."

Rahel is a woman of great spiritual and physical beauty. She loves the king dearly and their utter devotion to each other breeds jealously among the king's courtiers. She senses her precarious position, and with fatalistic expectation of doom clings to the king. As he prepares for a hunt she conveys her fears to him but insists that he not change his plans. As soon as he leaves, conspiring knights rush into her boudoir with drawn swords. They counter her pleas with accusations that the king's love for her has led to his failure in war, and is bringing ruin to his kingdom.

Rahel turns to her assassins. Her eyes aflame with superhuman love, she urges them to thrust their swords into her bosom if it is her death which alone can redeem her beloved Alfons. Struck by her extraordinary beauty, the knights hesitate. In a flash, Rahel snatches a sword from the hand of the chief conspirator, and thrusts it into her heart. Soundlessly, she falls to the ground.

"Rahel!" the king's cry resounds in the halls of the castle. When he reaches Rahel and takes her in his arms, passion for vengeance mingles with grief on his face. But the Jewess whispers with her last breath, "No revenge!" It was she who killed herself out of love for him: no one should be blamed for it. He should now instead reunite with his people in friendship and peace.

The message of love and forgiveness in the voice of the Jewess was intended to work in favor of Jews, to plead for tolerance. Continuing Lessing's endeavors of more than a hundred years before, Günther Walling employed the same means to the same end. Recha of Lessing captivated German audiences with her innocent trust in human kindness in 1779. The same values were patently meaningful in 1887. And the need for the cry of tolerance toward Jews was just as urgent during the last decades of the nineteenth century as it had been in the eighteenth. Religious intolerance had kept the Jew behind ghetto walls in the pre-Lessing era; now the rise of nationalist intolerance threatened to expel him from the state. It was an age that historians today call the pre-Nazi period: its extreme nationalistic and anti-Semitic reverberations proved to be the launching pad of Nazism. The century, which began with Enlightenment and Reason fighting for Jewish emancipation, ended as an age of reaction and regression. The valiant, well-meaning efforts of literary men with their various positive portrayals of Jews only succeeded in staving off the catastrophe a little longer.

4

The Romantic Casualty

> "By the scalp of Abraham," said Prince John, "yonder Jewess must be the very model of that perfection whose charms drove frantic the wisest king that ever lived! What sayest thou, Prior Aymer?"
>
> "The Rose of Sharon and the Lily of the Valley," answered the Prior, in a sort of snuffling tone; "but your Grace must remember she is still but a Jewess."[1]

The English beauty that adorned the stands at a tourney or the dais of a banquet hall had flaxen hair and angelic blue eyes; a rosy complexion complemented her wholesome gentility. "The very model of perfection" in the above quotation, however, had strikingly white skin set off by raven black hair, and eyes that bespoke sadness and sensuality. You would not expect to meet her at English tourneys or banquets. You would see her in paintings depicting biblical beauties, great dramatic figures of the past—beguiling, fascinating, haunting. You would read lyric poems or elegies about her, or dream about her when your mood mellowed and filled you with secret yearning. She is not just a woman: she is a phenomenon. She is the Jewess at her most romantic.

She is Rebecca of York at a twelfth-century tourney between Saxon and Norman knights in Walter Scott's *Ivanhoe* (1820). What is she doing there? The excitement her appearance creates testifies not only to her extraordinary beauty but to the incongruity of her presence, and the striking quality of both. The Forbidden Woman, she is Madonna-like: "a noble and commanding figure, the long white veil, in which she was shrouded, overshadowing rather than concealing, the elegance and majesty of her shape." A sinner in the garb of a saint, Rebecca represents that most heartbreaking of fictional Jewesses, the dream-girl of nineteenth-century Romantics.

George du Maurier describes her in his own version as

> a type that sometimes, just now and again, can be so pathetically noble and beautiful in a woman, so suggestive of chastity and the most passionate love combined—love conjugal and filial and maternal—love that implies all the big practical obligations and responsibilities of human life, that the mere term "Jewess" (and especially its French equivalent) brings to my mind, some vague, mysterious, exotically poetic image of all I love best in a woman. I find myself dreaming of Rebecca of York, as I used to dream of her in English class at Brossard's where I pitied poor Ivanhoe for his misplaced constancy.[2]

George du Maurier, in *The Martian* (1897), fashioned his romantic Jewess, the lovely black-haired Leah Gibson, on the pattern of Rebecca, as did all other novelists of the Romantic school. Their heartbreaking beauty notwithstanding, the Rebeccas of this genre are tragic victims of their Jewishness, casualties of their confrontation with a Christian.

Walter Scott did not create Rebecca: she is a romanticized version of Abigail, an "improved" model to suit the sophistication of the period. Because of the refined sensitivities of the age, the story of her having loved and lost the Christian of her destiny is couched in terms less harsh, her tragedy stated with less brutality.

The nineteenth century is described by historians as a reaction to the Enlightenment and its values, a virtual blacklash to the Age of Reason. For the Jew it was much more than an Age of Un-Reason. The nineteenth century created a new epoch in Jewish history. It brought the Jew to the height of his aspirations and also to the depth of his despair. In mid-century the Jews of Europe realized their most cherished desire: they were finally recognized as citizens in the countries of their birth. Having their civil equality confirmed allowed them with one blissful stroke to cancel out centuries of abuse and suffering. Yet, at the same time, the nineteenth century declared the Jews an alien "race," and recommended their bodily removal from Europe. It legitimized Jew-hatred by forming official anti-Jewish political parties; enthusiastically it endorsed and voted their candidates into high offices. It even granted an aura of intellectuality to Jew-hatred by giving it a fancy name—anti-Semitism. Anti-Semitism became a legitimate movement during the latter decades of the century, along with other "isms."

But the century of Un-Reason also gave birth to Jewish nationalism which cradled political Zionism. It prepared the ground for the ingathering of the exiles the world over, for modern Jewish settlement in Palestine, and eventually for the establishment of the Jewish State.

The nineteenth century thus held the seeds of Jewish destruction and rebirth. The seeds of modern anti-Semitism produced the Holocaust, Jewry's greatest catastrophe. And the seeds of modern Zionism sprouted into the State of Israel, Jewry's Messianic hope-fulfillment.

The cataclysmic events of the twentieth century were preceded by the social and political ferment of the nineteenth. Jewry was caught in the grip of these forces and the image of the Jewess in many literary works reflected the crises. These Jewish heroines are discussed in the next chapter. The Jewesses of the Romantics, modelled after Rebecca, seem, however, largely unaffected by these changes. They continue their role within the established pattern as passive tools of social and literary convention.

The times are reflected solely in the Jewess's continued alienation and in the increasing role of baptism in many stories, together with the Jewess's rejection despite her baptism. But the Jewess herself is not altered. She is the same beautiful, desirable, suffering sex object, who, like an object, is swept away by the current. She does not face up to it, protest or struggle against it, but rather she allows herself to submerge and often to drown. She is, invariably, a casualty.

Walter Scott's Rebecca, the prototype of this Jewess image, is cast in a complex plot of courtly love and hate superimposed on a twelfth-century English milieu. England is torn by strife between Saxons and Normans. Crusaders and outlaws roam the countryside. Despised by all groups, protected by none, the Jews are at the whim of friend and foe, and are constantly at pains to placate both with payments of ransom or tribute—in whatever form their meager coins are extorted from them. The goodwill of an occasional noble knight offers a rare measure of protection, or dignity.

Such a knight is Ivanhoe. His nobility of spirit is as evident in his generous consideration toward Jews as in his devotion to the fair Rowena. Circumstances, however, throw Ivanhoe and the Jewess Rebecca together. Her ministrations restore him to health after he is wounded; his gentility and valor win her heart. They are drawn to one another with a depth of feeling neither can ignore. Conveniently, before their feelings lead to impossible conclusions, the plot contrives to separate them.

Ivanhoe returns to champion Rebecca and save her from death, but he weds the Christian Rowena. Rebecca, a day after their wedding, requests a private audience with Rowena and offers her a gift—a silver casket containing jewelry of great value. She will have no more need of it: she and her father are leaving England for lands where more protection is extended to their people. She will no longer wear jewels; her life henceforth will be dedicated to another master, a comforter to whose will she has chosen to devote herself.

> "Have you then convents, to one of which you mean to retire?" asked Rowena.
>
> "No, lady," said the Jewess; "but among our people, since the time of Abraham downwards, have been women who have devoted their thoughts to Heaven, and their actions to works of kindness to men—tending the sick, feeding the hungry, and relieving the distressed. Among these will Rebecca be numbered. Say this to thy lord, should he chance to inquire after the fate of her whose life he saved."
>
> There was an involuntary tremor on Rebecca's voice, and a tenderness of accent, which perhaps betrayed more than she would willingly have expressed. She hastened to bid Rowena adieu.
>
> "Farewell," she said. "May He who made both Jew and Christian shower down on you His choicest blessing!"[3]

Like a true martyr, Rebecca retires into self-imposed celibacy. Having loved and lost, the Jewess withdraws gracefully, her dignity and chastity intact. English Romanticism failed to produce social tools for the solution of the Jewess-Christian dilemma. Despite her heroic dimensions, Rebecca the Jewess is unacceptable as partner in marriage to Ivanhoe the Christian. Nineteenth-century English society continues its ambivalence towards the Jew.

Ever since the repeal of the Jew Bill (in 1753) which would have granted citizenship to all British Jews on application to Parliament, the controversy and the agitation for the measure continued. Several leading Sephardic families, the first Jews to resettle in England in the seventeenth century, seeing the public pressure against it, lost hope of ever attaining full equality with their Christian neighbors. They gave up Judaism and joined the English Church. The poignancy of this occurrence is evident when we consider that these families originated as Marranos (secret Jews), having escaped from the Inquisition in

Spain and Portugal two hundred years before. They then adhered to their ancestral faith at the risk of their lives, and now when much less was at stake, they despaired of it.

Rebecca of *Ivanhoe* reflects this mood of the times. After narrowly escaping death brought on by religious intolerance and rejection by Ivanhoe, Rebecca and her father leave the country.

Could the script have been written differently? Was this the only solution permitted by the convention of the times? Could the Christian hero who defied convention by championing her cause have gone one step further and married the Jewess?

William M. Thackeray was offended by Scott's solution to the Rebecca-Ivanhoe romance and, in order to rectify the injustice, wrote his own version of the love story. In the introduction to his novel *Rebecca and Rowena* (1850) Thackeray explains his reasons:

> My dear Rebecca, daughter of Isaac of York, was always in my mind.... Nor can I ever believe that such a woman, so admirable, so tender, so heroic, so beautiful, could disappear altogether before such another woman as Rowena, that vapid, flaxen-headed creature, who is in my humble opinion, unworthy of Ivanhoe, and unworthy of her place as heroine. Had both of them got their right it ever seemed to me that Rebecca would have had the husband, and Rowena would have gone off to a convent and shut herself up, where I, for one, would never have taken the trouble of inquiring for her.
>
> But after all she married Ivanhoe ... And must the Disinherited Knight, whose blood has been fired by the suns of Palestine, and whose heart has been warmed in the company of the tender and beautiful Rebecca, sit down contented for life by the side of such a frigid piece of propriety as that icy, faultless, prim miminy-piminy Rowena? Forbid it, Fate, forbid it, poetical Justice![4]

Thackeray's Ivanhoe does marry Rebecca—after it is revealed that the latter has secretly converted to Christianity. As to the "vapid, flaxen-headed creature," she is justly abandoned to a fate of chastity and hopelessness in a medieval convent.

Thackeray's cure is worse than the disease he proposes to heal: his "solution" provides an even clearer example and proof of the malaise. The impasse of Jewish-Christian relations generated by age-old ambivalencies could scarcely have found a more graphic illustration than Thackery's well-intentioned efforts at solution. In order to give it a happy ending, Thackeray felt compelled to change the story: in order to find happiness with a Christian, a Jewess must cease to be a Jewess. But then the problem does not exist in the first place; there is no dilemma, and no need for a solution. A Rebecca who chooses baptism is not a Rebecca at all. Her raison d'être, her very essence, is negated by such a premise.

Scott himself had taken notice of the problem and justified his own attitude in the introduction to a later edition of *Ivanhoe:*

> The character of the fair Jewess found so much favor in the eyes of some fair readers, that the writer was censured because, when arranging the fates of the characters of the drama, he had not assigned the hand of Wilfred to Rebecca, rather than the less interesting Rowena. But, not to mention that the prejudices of the age rendered such a union almost impossible, the Author may, in passing, observe, that he thinks a character of a highly virtuous and lofty stamp is degraded rather than exalted by an attempt to reward virtue with temporal prosperity.[5]

"Prejudice of the age"—which? The medieval period when the "drama" takes place, or Scott's nineteenth century? An author may, however, be forgiven for ignoring contemporary reality as long as he faithfully adheres to literary convention: Rebecca, the true Romantic heroine "of a highly virtuous and lofty stamp," must remain on her pedestal, as do all other stereotypical Jewesses. Not even one is rewarded by "temporal prosperity."

Beautiful Rebecca Gratz, a prominent Philadelphia socialite and great friend of Washington Irving, served as Scott's model for his beautiful Rebecca. The popular member of a large American literary circle, Rebecca Gratz never married. She was a social welfare activist, and was admired by Jews and Gentiles alike for her untiring efforts on behalf of her fellow citizens, as well as for her remarkable charm and intelligence. She was the initiator of the Jewish Sunday School system, the founder of the first Jewish orphanage in the United States and of other pioneer projects. Washington Irving, on a visit to Scott in 1817, spoke with admiration about the American Jewess's extraordinary qualities. When *Ivanhoe* was published in 1819, Scott sent a copy of the novel to Irving and wanted to know what the American writer thought of the Jewish heroine. He wrote: "How do you like your Rebecca? Does the Rebecca I have pictured compare with the pattern given?"

Two other fascinating nineteenth-century Jewesses served as models for Romantic heroines. One was lovely Rebecca Franks, daughter of a great Jewish American patriot, Jacob Franks, after whom Paul Leicester Ford fashioned the title character of his novel *Janice Meredith: A Story of the American Revolution (1899).* The other was an unnamed mysterious Jewess who so fascinated Nathanial Hawthorne at a party in London that the American writer made her a central character in his romance *The Marble Faun* (1860). Dark, mysterious Miriam, although the subject of a somewhat unusual story line, is another perfect specimen of the romanticized Jewess stereotype. Brilliant and beautiful, Hawthorne's Jewess is also a helpless victim of the doom that befalls the love of a Jew and a Christian.

Another American, Herman Melville, in his narrative poem *Clarel* (1876), approached the Christian-Jewess dilemma on two levels. While Old World stereotypes persisting in American literature influenced his expectations, New World liberalism shaped his attitudes. Superimposing the former on the latter, Melville created a dual approach to the problem. Although the plot and the female characters reflect the stereotyped pattern, his treatment of the issue reflects a liberal view of the Jew. This liberal view may very well reflect Melville's experiences in a merchant house in Manhattan and consequent knowledge of real "Jews."

Clarel is an American student on pilgrimage to Christian holy places in Palestine. Among his more memorable experiences in the Holy Land is his meeting a beautiful Jewish girl. The pious young pilgrim is captivated by gentle Ruth's innocent loveliness:

> She looked a legate to insure
> That Paradise was possible
> Now and hereafter. 'Twas the grace
> of Nature's dawn: an Eve-like face
> And Nereid eyes with virgin spell
> Candid as day, yet baffling quite
> Like day, through unreserve of light.
> A dove she seemed, a temple dove,
> Born in the temple or its grove,
> And nurtured there. But deeper viewed,
> What was it that looked part amiss?
> A bit impaired? What lack of peace?
> Enforced suppression of a mood,
> Regret with yearning intertwined,
> And secret protest of a virgin mind.
> Hebrew the profile, every line;
> But as haven fringed with palm,
> Which Indian reefs embay from harm,
> Belulled as in the vase of wine—
> Red budded corals in remove,
> Peep coy through quietudes above;
> So through clear olive of the skin,

And features finely Hagarene;
Its way a tell-tale blush did win—
A tint which unto Israel's sand
Blabbed of June in some far clover land.[6]

Clarel befriends Ruth and she turns out to be an American who, together with her parents, has emigranted to the Holy Land. Ruth introduces him to her family, and Clarel becomes a frequent visitor. The American Jews are happy to see him: he reminds them of America, the "Gentile land where nature's wreath exhales the first creation's breath." Friendship with Clarel ripens into love on the part of Ruth, and into affection on the part of the parents, especially the mother, Agar. Clarel's love for Ruth, the "dove-like maiden" is coupled with deep attachment to Agar; to him she is the mother he had never known. Within the circle of these Jews, Clarel experiences familial warmth for the first time in his life:

Clarel, bereft while still but young,
Mother or sister had not known;
To him now first in life was shown,
In Agar's frank demeanor kind,
What charm to woman may belong
When by natural bent inclined
To goodness in domestic play:
On earth no better thing than this—
It canonizes very clay:
Madonna hence thy worship is.[7]

Ruth and Clarel get engaged, and all the family look forward happily to the future. One day, while Clarel is on a visit to Mt. Zion, Arab marauders attack the Jewish home, murder the father, and burn down the house. Upon his return Clarel finds that the house of mourning, in which Agar and Ruth according to Jewish custom sit grieving for seven days, is barred to him, the non-Jew. Neighbors tell him that only "Hebrews" may enter at a time like this. Disconsolate, Clarel goes on a pilgrimage to the Dead Sea to spend the days that separate him from the girl he loves.

Returning, he passes a burial ground where a funeral is about to take place. He discovers that the shrouded bodies near the open graves are those of Agar and Ruth. Agar has died of grief over her husband's death, and Ruth over rejection by Clarel, who she assumed had abandoned her. Clarel cries out in agony:

O blind, blind, barren universe!
Now I am like a bough turn down,

And must wither, cloud or sun!—
Had I been near, this had not been.
Do spirits look down upon this scene?—
. . . Take me, take me, Death!
Where Ruth is gone, me thither whirl,
Where'er it be![8]

The Christian hero's frank grief over the Jewesses' death humanizes the Jewess figure. Melville's sympathetic attitude towards Jews is most evident, however, in his treatment of the male character. Deviating from the stereotypical pattern, the father figure here is youthful and positive. And he has a wife, a feature that makes him seem decidedly more human than all the old, ugly, and lonely Jewish fathers that precede him.

Indeed, the mother in this narrative is not only present but plays a central role. In a striking innovation, the Jewess image is split into two elements: virginity and eroticism are embodied in Ruth the daughter, and the Madonna aspect in Agar the mother. The young Christian is in love with both women. The twin role necessitates their simultaneous deaths and twin burial. Both women become victim to convention: as romantic heroines and as Jewesses.

Although Sephardic Jews had emigrated from the Netherlands and settled in New York, Philadelphia, and Baltimore in the seventeenth century, and many Jews from England settled in seaboard cities of the South, socializing with Jews was limited in Melville's America. The German-Jewish immigrants who in mid-century roamed the Midwest as itinerant peddlers were small in number, and were swallowed up by the vast expanse of the country. They were insignificant as social phenomena at the time. The majority of Americans had little contact with Jews in the flesh and continued to perpetuate the preconception of Jew as biblical patriarch or the devil incarnate. Most American writers depicted the Jew as Abraham or Judas; the Jewess was matriarch Sarah, Rebecca, or Rachel, Deborah the Prophetess, or Esther the Queen. Even during the last decades of the century, when east European immigration more than quadrupled the Jewish population of the United States, the literary image of the Jew remained unchanged. The poverty-stricken Yiddish-speaking east European Jews concentrated mainly in New York, and their presence was scarcely felt by the wide American public. The stereotypes persevered.

Russian literature, especially in its earlier stages, was also an uncritical heir to western literary traditions. The image of the Jewess found its way into Russian drama, novels, and poetry, within the familiar framework of the Jewess-Christian pattern.

Under Czars who committed themselves to a brutal elimination of the "Jewish problem," the second half of the nineteenth century was a succession of nightmares in the life of Russian Jewry. Incarcerated in the Pale where crowding, poverty, and despair were routine facts of life, the Jewish woman filled the role of mother, wife and often breadwinner. More often than not she was the single bulwark of the family against the determination of the Russian authorities to make good on the Czar's promise.

Seldom was she seen beyond the "shtetl." The boundaries of that ghetto were ruthlessly guarded by ever-increasing restrictions. Until the Revolution it was the rare, privileged Jew who was permitted to travel beyond the Pale, and then only on important business. Women did not have "important business." The Jewish woman, from the day of its establishment in 1795, until its abolition in 1917, did not step outside her ghetto in the Russian Pale.

What then served as model for the numerous literary works which placed the Jewish heroine in a central role? Besides biblical images, there was a vast depository of works by English, French, and German writers of the Romantic school, at this time the major source of Russian literary inspiration.

The love theme of Jewess and Christian, and her eventual rejection, is popular with several nineteenth-century Russian writers. Anton Chekhov's play *Ivanov* (1887–89) casts the lovely, intelligent, and sensitive Jewess, Sara, in the role of the starry-eyed romantic who meets and falls in love with a Russian nobleman, Nikolai Ivanov. When he tells her to follow him, she willingly leaves her family and friends, and goes with the young Christian to his estate in a distant part of the country. Sara is baptized, changes her name to Anna, and becomes Ivanov's wife. She is deliriously happy with her love and does not reflect on the personal sacrifice she made for its sake.

Her happiness does not last however. The Russian nobleman tires of the complex, sensitive Jewess, and starts to attend soirées at the homes of local gentry where he cannot take her. She does not belong. The gradual withdrawal of his love is keenly obvious to the sensitive young woman and she suffers deeply. She loses interest in living. Her appetite fails and she becomes fatally ill with consumption. The young doctor who treats her tries in vain to cheer her up. She speaks to him of her loneliness and dejection, and of the change that has come over her life:

> You know, doctor, I am beginning to think that Fate has cheated me. Lots of people who are probably no better than me are happy, and

> yet they haven't had to pay for their happiness. But I have paid! . . . Nikolai is a remarkable man. . . . Oh, he was wonderful! I fell in love with him at first sight. . . . He said: come with me . . . and I did. I cut every tie that bound me to my old life . . . and I went. But things are different now. Now he goes off to the Lebedevs to amuse himself with other women and I sit here in the garden and listen to the owl screeching. . . .[9]

A suspicion of her husband's infidelity makes her reflect on her past. Her life turns into a lingering death. Nikolai amuses himself at the Lebedevs, a Russian upper-class family of vulgar tastes and ordinary women. He advises the men in the company not to marry Jewesses but to stick to local Christian girls "who do not sparkle, and do not talk a lot." Anna is dying slowly, by degrees.

After her death, the beautiful, delicate Anna is remembered with fondness by Nikolai's uncle who used to play duets with her on the violin, and with grief by the doctor who had fallen in love with her. But Nikolai marries soon the earthy daughter of the Lebedevs. The encounter with the Jewess is a thing of the past. Her relevance? Nothing more than a small ripple caused by the drop of a tiny pebble in the pool.

Turgenev's Jewess is the sad but striking Susanna, the protagonist of the short story "Hapless Girl," a Jewish orphan converted to Christianity and placed in a Christian foster home to receive a pious Christian upbringing.

Like Jewish orphans in other parts of Christendom, Susanna was apparently made a ward of the state and forcibly baptized. Her foster family grudgingly tolerates the outsider, probably for the kopeks her upkeep brings to them. She is a bright, sensitive girl and soon feels the full force of her alienation. She is unloved but yearns for love with the passion of her "Jewish" temperament. Susanna falls in love with Michel, her foster brother. But Michel treats her with cold courtesy, like the rest of her foster family. Where is she to turn? Her Jewish past is a closed book. Her Christian future carries only the promise of rejection. Realizing the hopelessness of her situation, the alienated Jewess kills herself.

Baptism was a central factor in Christian-Jewish relations in Czarist Russia. It was a perpetual objective of the government: the conversion of the Jews to Russian Orthodoxy offered the only hope for a permanent elimination of the Jewish problem. Jews were a vexing issue ever since Catherine the Great "inherited" them, together with segments of Poland in its partition among the major powers—Russia, Austria, and Germany. Up to the last decade of the eighteenth century, when with the partition of Poland about one million Jews found themselves under Russian occupation, no Jew was admitted to Russia. Totally unprepared to cope with this unexpected development, first Catherine and then every subsequent Czar attempted to solve the problem of the Jews on Russian soil with a different plan. Catherine devised the Pale—a ghetto-like reservation which enclosed the Jews within confines they were not permitted to cross. Isolating them, limiting their influence, and stunting their growth was her proposed solution. Her descendants invented other means, such as exorbitant taxes and other financial extortions; prohibitions against most modes of livelihood, education, and Jewish religious or cultural expression; compulsory draft at a brutally young age for brutally long periods; periodic expulsions; organized pogroms; kidnapping and forcible baptism of children. Kidnapping for the sake of baptism was openly condoned by both the Russian Church and the government.

The Jews of Russia clung tenaciously to their faith despite these repressive measures. While in western Europe Enlightenment and civil liberties induced the Jews to assimilate and convert to Christianity, harsh repression in Russia produced the reverse. It was only during the last decades of the nineteenth century that a trend towards secularization made itself felt within Russian Jewry, and then it nearly ripped the hitherto homogeneous community apart. The secularists were bitterly denounced by the rest of the community. Individuals choosing the path of assimilation had to reach it through renunciation of all ties with their family and friends. While the Jew in western Europe was born into a world of civil liberties and economic opportunities granted to his father and grandfather, the Jew in Russia was just beginning to dream about these freedoms and privileges, knowing that if they were ever to be granted to him, he would have to fight for them. Secularization was the first step in that struggle. It was also the first step in the strife within Russian Jewry.

The strife is reflected in the writings of Jewish authors of the period. But the Christian world was largely unaware of the inner Jewish turmoil; it was unaware of the inner Jewish world. It continued to portray the idealized, romantic Jewess in the setting of the Middle Ages or the Bible, as in works by French, German, and English Romantics. Scott's Rebecca found an echo in Mikhail Lermontov's Noemi (in *The Spaniards* discussed in a later chapter), in Ivan Lazhechnikov's Rebekka in the play *Daughter of the Jew* (1849), and in Nestor Kukolnik's Rakhel in both *The Statue of Kristoph in Riga* (1852) and *Prince Daniel Dimitrievich Kholmskii* (1852). Byron's *Hebrew Melodies*—"She Walks in Beauty," "Jephtha's Daughter," "Herod's Lament for Marianne," "By the Rivers of Babylon . . ."—(1815) were echoed by Lermontov's *Hebrew Melodies* (1830), bemoaning the beauty and tragic fate of biblical Jewesses. Friedrich Hebbel's biblical drama, *Judith* (1840), has its parallel in Alexander Pushkin's lyric poems "Judith" and "Christ Is Risen, O My Rebekka!" Alexander Kuprin's Etliya in the short story *The Jewess* (1904) is a composite of Old and New Testament heroines.

Only Chekhov and Turgenev hinted at the inner conflict of the Jew by means of the context in which they placed their stereotyped Jewesses: the tragic consequences of baptism are portrayed realistically enough. But there is no hint of the change that was taking place within the psyche of the Jew—the growing awareness of self-worth, and the inner conflict between ambition for secularization and a revived sense of Jewish identity.

In the complex world of Jewish mentality both were happening. While Jewish young began to wave the banner of "progress," which meant abandonment of tradition and adherence to Socialist ideals—in short, assimilation—it also waved the banner of Jewish nationalism, return to Zion and pioneering in Palestine, which meant abandoning the Jewish tradition in quite another sense—reinterpreting the concept of Judaism as a matter not of religion but of nationality and culture. Only Chirikov, in his play *The Jews,* portrays a woman who reflects the modern Jewess which evolved from the stereotypical sex object.

Ironically several Jewish writers of the period borrowed the stereotypical image and plot in order to depict Jewish reality. Karl Emil Franzos and Alfred Meissner, for instance, in their attempt to articulate the conflict between baptism and Jewish tradition, employed the Jewess-Christian pattern without subjective modification. In *Judith Trachtenberg* (1819), Franzos presents the regulation lovely Jewess in a Galician ghetto who falls in love with a Polish count, and, ignoring the pleas of her father, abandons faith and family. She follows the Christian to his country, but soon the Pole tires of her and deserts her. Broken in spirit, Judith becomes fatally ill. Finally she summons enough determination to return home. Making her way towards the town, she is too weak to reach the walls of the ghetto but staggers instead into the Jewish cemetery and there collapses, lifeless, among the tombs.

The grave as a symbol of Judaism for those who abandoned it was popular with Jewish writers. In Alfred Meissner's poem "The Jewess" the anonymous Jewish heroine follows a blond Austrian officer to Venice just as compulsively as Judith followed the Polish count. He promises her a life of carefree pleasure and showers her with tokens of his love. At home, the entire Jewish community performs the rites of mourning and her family sits "shiva," the seven days of bereavement, as if she were dead. Even her grave is dug. It awaits her as surely as the doom that awaits every Jewess who reaches out for the love of a Christian. "Das Grab das wartet"—the grave, it awaits—is the poem's theme and haunting refrain.

The Jewish grave awaits while she basks in the Mediterranean sunshine, and while she lolls on the gondola in her lover's arms. It awaits silently while she laughs, and sings, and shrieks with delight. It awaits while the sunshine fades and the laughter freezes on the Jewess's lips. The Austrian officer has disappeared, and she is left alone, friendless, destitute, and pregnant. In vain she searches the shore daily in hopes of his promised return. She bears the child but it soon dies, and nothing but a searing memory remains of the enticing encounter. Her Jewish past is the only possible haven, and the Jewess gropes her way back to the outskirts of her town, to the cemetery. There she tumbles into the open grave that has awaited her.

Eventual doom like a magnet draws the helpless Romantic Jewess. Her entire world is built on love, other realities do not penetrate her realm of concern. She is passive in the face of events that powerfully affect her surroundings. As if she were protected by a charmed circle of romance, she stands aloof from the realities shaping the history of her era.

Romantic to the core, she is passive also in the face of her love and its rejection. Like the Madonna that she is, the Rebecca of the Romantics suffers nobly her rejection by the Christian; she does nothing else about it. Unless a hurt and dignified fade-out, so superbly executed by Walter Scott's Rebecca; or death of heartbreak, elegantly carried out by Ruth and Agar of Melville, and Anna of Chekhov; or suicide committed by Turgenev's Susanna; or an escape into madness, achieved by Lermontov's Noemi, can be called "doing something" about a thing so basic to her being.

Perhaps the grave as a recurrent motif is a hint of realism. Symbolizing the Jewish past in assimilationist perspective, the grave as ultimate answer in the Jewess-Christian dilemma is perhaps an indication of things to come.

The next stage in the evolution of the Jewess image shows the Jewish heroine's growing awareness of Jewish identity, together with her self-awareness as a person. She breaks the shackles of the romantic image and its compelling "feminine" passivity, and assumes a positive role as a symbol of Jewry's critical choices at the crossroads of the modern era.

Curiously, this modern Jewess, and modern woman, emerged as an offshoot of a uniquely romanticized "sex object," the creation of nineteenth-century French life and literature—the "belle Juive," the Jewish courtesan. A unique phenomenon, the beautiful Jewish courtesan of French letters encompasses elements of the Virgin-Madonna simultaneously with the passion and fierce individuality characteristic of the Jewish woman—elements out of which her modern equivalent eventually evolved.

5

La Belle Juive: The Jewish Courtesan

> There is in the words "belle Juive" a very special sexual signification, one quite different from that contained in the words "beautiful Rumanian," "beautiful Greek," or "beautiful American," for example. This phrase carries an aura of rape and massacre. The "beautiful Jewess" is she whom the Cossacks under the czars dragged by her hair through the streets of her burning village. And the special works which are given over to accounts of flagellation reserve a place of honor for the Jewess.[1]

> In France it is extremely rare, if not impossible to find the thirty famed perfections of feminine beauty. . . . Esther would have carried off the prize in the seraglio: she possessed the thirty beauties harmoniously blended.

> Esther looked delicate but was remarkably vigorous; she attracted attention through a characteristic captured in the most artistic manner by Raphael in his figures, for Raphael was the painter who studied the Jewish beauty most closely and portrayed it most strikingly.[2]

To irresistible Esther the "perfection of feminine beauty" was a birthright: her mother was a Jewess, a descendant of a "race" which originated in the "cradle of mankind."

But beauty alone is not the element which distinguishes Esther from other women, let alone from other courtesans. She has a special quality of spirit, a loftiness of soul, which elevates her beauty to the superhuman plane where objects of adoration stand.

Esther proves worthy of idealization. She is a courtesan. But for the sake of the man she loves, she gives up a life of pleasure and pampering by infatuated males, and enters a convent to undergo spiritual transformation. Her devotion borders on saintliness and earns the admiration of her tutors, including the Mother Superior. Esther's purity of soul and human love transcend the memories of her past; she inspires reverence in worldly, even cynical, observers.

But her sacrifice and total spiritual commitment prove futile. With the insight and maturity acquired through suffering, Esther realizes that the noble lover for whose sake she chose to inflict pain on herself would be better off without her. Without a moment's hesitation, Esther now makes the ultimate sacrifice for love: she commits suicide, so that her lover may marry the woman she believes is better for him.

The Romantic period could pay womanhood no greater accolade than that which Balzac chose to award through the figure of Esther. The heroism of total commitment, a virtue admired by Balzac and his age, found embodiment in this fragile yet indefatigable Jewess.

In that sense, Rachel of Guy de Maupassant's *Mademoiselle Fifi*[3] parallels Esther's role. This "belle Juive" becomes the symbol of patriotism, a virtue of utmost value in post-war France. One of five courtesans brought to a castle near Rouen to entertain Prussian officers during the Franco-Prussian War of 1871, Rachel is picked by the protagonist ("Mademoiselle Fifi") as a companion for the evening. During the merry drinking that follows, the Prussian repeatedly insults France in spite of the girls' protestations. But the Jewess is the only one to rise to the defense of France's honor: she snatches a knife from the table and fatally stabs the officer. Leaping through the window, she manages to elude a whole battalion of Prussian soldiers sent to arrest her. Symbolically, her haven is the belfry of the church. And when the Prussians order the patriotic old priest to toll the bells for the officer's funeral, he goes against his vow to keep the bells silent until the liberation of France; he obeys in order to protect the "belle Juive."

After the liberation of France Rachel becomes a French heroine. Her past as a courtesan does not prevent people from hailing her for her bravery and an upright young Frenchman from marrying her. Unlike Esther, Rachel lives to enjoy the rewards of her virtue: honored by all, she becomes integrated into respectable French society.

The choice of Jewish courtesans as symbols of outstanding virtues—purity, self-sacrifice, courage, and patriotism—reveals attitudes toward courtesans, and toward Jewesses. While in other cultures a personification of relevant moral and emotional values by a courtesan world be incongruous, in French literature it was a plausible choice. In other cultures considered with disdain, in nineteenth-century France the courtesan was a romanticized figure of considerable power, even of tacit respect. The Jewess image, with its associations of irresistible charm, eroticism, tenderness, and warmth, rendered the role of courtesan almost a logical one for the Jewess in French belles lettres of the period.

And if the Jewess was chosen as a literary courtesan, she was to be a courtesan with a halo, the cream of courtesans, even as in the case of Balzac's Esther, a courtesan-saint. Strangely, without a trace of incongruity, the belle Juive in her eroticism retained an air of virginity and a Madonna-like quality. Despite the obvious implications of her profession, the Jewess-image remained intact: each of the three basic elements found expression in her role as courtesan. She was, in fact, the Madonna as courtesan.

For French writers the gift of feminity was most fully realized in the romanticized role of the courtesan. While others offered the delightful Jewess only to princes and noblemen, French authors, in their liberalism, presented her as courtesan for the pleasure of the public at large. Even though eventually she became attached to one privileged man, initially her abundant endowments of love were not limited to the chosen few.

Raphaële of Maupassant's *La Maison Tellier* (1881), for instance, was the darling of that famous bordello, an eagerly sought-after solace to men in all walks of life. All, no matter what their background, noble or common, chose the Jewess in preference to the other courtesans of the place. It was not her subtle erotic magnetism which distinguished the Jewess and rendered her the favorite but rather her kindness and sympathy, traits derived from the Mary image.

The Mary complex manifested in the form of courtesan is a most fortunate characterization. The triple aspect of her womanhood—virginity, eroticism, and motherhood—appealed to the masses of Mary's followers with a symbolic sexuality similar to that offered by the tender, understanding, and sympathetic courtesan. While dogmatic claims of Mary's perpetual virginity revealed the Church's effort to overcome what it believed was the inherent sinfulness of womanhood, worshippers paid tribute precisely to the symbolic sexuality of the Virgin Mother. While the Church and its Fathers insisted on the dogma of *virgo concepit, virgo peperit, virgo permansit,* the multitudes of the faithful insisted on adoring the Woman—the representative of

Love. It was to the Woman they had flocked ever since the early Middle Ages with supplications and gifts; it was to the Madonna they brought confession offerings, and it was to the Lady they built altars and cathedrals. It was the lure of love and maternal tenderness that attracted the doubters, the sufferers, the hopeful. It was the instinctive yearning for the closeness of Woman that made the adoration of Mary universal—and the attraction of the courtesan irresistible.

Henry Adams, in his *Mont-Saint-Michel and Chartres* (1904) traces the history of this worship of woman in the architecture of the cathedral. "The proper study of mankind is woman," he concludes, "and, by common agreement since the time of Adam, it is the most complex and arduous. The study of Our Lady, as shown by the art of Chartres, leads directly back to Eve, and lays bare the whole subject of sex."[4]

Woman as representative of love stood above law and even religion, and Mary, the ultimate woman, similarly defied law and even theology, for the sake of love.

> True it was, although one should not say it jestingly, that the Virgin embarrassed the Trinity; and perhaps this was the reason, behind all other excellent reasons, why men loved and adored her with a passion such as no other deity has ever inspired. . . .
>
> The convulsive hold which Mary to this day maintains over human imagination—as you can see at Lourdes—was due much less to her power of saving soul or body than to her sympathy with people who suffered under law—divine or human—justly or unjustly, by accident or design, by decree of God or by guile of Devil. . . . three hundred years later the Puritan reformers were not satisfied with abolishing her, but sought to abolish the woman altogether as the cause of evil in heaven and on earth. The Puritans abandoned the New Testament and the Virgin in order to go back to the beginning, and renew the quarrel with Eve.[5]

Just as the Puritans abolished the Mary image because of its close connection with Roman Catholicism and its unconventional appeal bordering on immorality, nineteenth-century French Romanticism translated it into the figure of the Jewish courtesan.

All other fictional Jewesses are in essence courtesans in disguise. Placed in different roles, supplied with different secondary features, their ultimate function without exception is that of dispensing love. Marlowe's Abigail, Racine's Bérénice, Lope de Vega's Raquel, Chekhov's Anna, Scott's Rebecca, Melville's Ruth are courtesans in the finest sense of that word. Even the Wandering Jewess, the mythical eternal woman, is primarily a sex symbol. In the various manifestations of her death-defying figure, the Wandering Jewess is but the immortal courtesan.

The creators of the "belle Juive" had in addition to Mary, another sacred literary precedent with which to authenticate their choice. Mary Magdalene of the New Testament served as a second source of inspiration: she was scriptural testimony to the redeemability of harlots. That special quality which in Christian view distinguishes the literary Jewess from other women, and the Jewish courtesan from other courtesans, prompted Mary Magdalene to recognize spiritual superiority in Jesus and abandon her ways of harlotry in his service.

Chateaubriand claims that Mary Magdalene and the other women of Jerusalem and Galilee who followed Jesus, and gave him encouragement and support, and displayed compassion for him, earned a place of honor and affection for Jewesses for all time. "A reflection of the light of God has remained with the Jewish woman," writes Chateaubriand. "They did not take part in the humiliation and torture of Christ; they showed compassion for him—a word of consolation. Therefore Jewish women were spared the malediction heaped upon Israel."[6]

If by their conduct toward Jesus Mary Magdalene and her companions spared the women of Israel from malediction, they also earned other positive advantages for the Jewess image. Wasn't it Mary Magdalene who was chosen to be the first witness to the Resurrection? Is she not regarded by tradition as the favorite disciple of Jesus whose kindness extended even to anointing his aching feet? Wasn't it Joan the wife of Chusa who gave him financial support when others reviled him? And Martha and Mary, the sisters of Lazarus, are not their names revered in Christendom for their infinite kindnesses toward Jesus? But the cult of the greatest reverence is reserved for the holy harlot who was believed to have been a medium of secret revelation. And this reverence of the Magdalene, the belief in her mystic power, was transferred to the fictional Jewess emerging as the "belle Juive."-

Such power emanates from Manette, the fascinating Jewish courtesan of Edmond and Jules de Goncourt's novel, *Manette Salomon* (1867). An artists' model, Manette exercises a strange impact on Coriolis, the young artist for whom she is posing. She is different from all the other models he has painted and the young man finds himself falling passionately in love with her.

Beneath her great beauty, Manette harbors a golden heart. She does not crave money and jewels; her greatest pleasure is to spend a quiet evening with her lover. And when he becomes ill, she devotedly nurses him back to health. Coriolis becomes her slave. His love for Manette is so all-absorbing that he subjugates even his art to his passion. More than an object of love, the courtesan becomes an object of adoration.

Victor Hugo's "belle Juive" is fully aware of her feminine power as a dominating force. She projects, like Manette Salomon in the second half of the novel, a mastery over the adoring male. She is the favorite sultana, the queen of the harem, and the sultan, the tyrannical master of thousands, is powerless before her every whim:

Haven't I, belle Juive, because of you
Depopulated my seraglio?
Do not request death to the rest.
Must each stroke of your fan
Be followed by that of an axe?

Yours are forever your rivals,
My spahis in turbans red
Racing non-stop
On steeds, sleek and swift
As rowers on their raft!

Yours are my people trembling!
Yours is Stamboul, which gathers
With a thousand bows erect
A fleet rocking on the ocean
At anchor rest!

Yours is Smyrna, and its houses new,
The shore which waves bitterly blanch
The Ganges which widows dread!
The Danube which five rivers through
Tumbles tousled into the sea!

Say, do you fear the daughters of Greece?
The pale lilies of Damanhour?
Or the ardent eyes of the negress,
Who, like a young tigress,
Leaps, roaring for love?

About you I care, adored Jewess,
Breast of ebony, face of rose!
You are not white, nor copper:
But it seems you're gilded,
with a ray of sun!

Don't call for storm any more
Upon these humble flowers;
Princess, enjoy your conquest in peace,
And don't insist that with every roll
Of your teardrop a head shall fall. . . .[7]

Contrasted with the theme of mystical power is that of compassion and all-encompassing love. Medieval French poems relating the miracles of the Virgin depict a picture of Mary strikingly similar to the portrait of the belle Juive. In these devotional songs Mary is the loving, compassionate, loyal woman—a lover of knights, circus-performers, farmers, and warriors. A tender, passionate, beautiful woman; a charming, demanding, possessive, and jealous lover whose anger flares as easily as her compassion, and who demands loyalty and love in measures perhaps even exceeding those in which she gives.

Henry Adams relates the incident of Mary's response to the change of plans of a young priest-to-be:

> One of her admirers, educated for the priesthood but not yet in full orders, was obliged by reasons of family interest to quit his career in order to marry. An insult like this was more than Mary could endure, and she gave the young man a lesson he never forgot:
>
> With anger flashing in her eyes
> Answers the Queen of Paradise:
> "Tell me, tell me! you of old
> Loved me once with love untold;
> Why now throw me aside?
> Tell me, tell me! Where a bride
> Kinder or fairer have you won?. . .
> Wherefore, wherefore, wretched one,
> Deceived, betrayed, misled, undone,
> Leave me for a creature mean,
> Me, who am of Heaven the Queen?
> Can you make a worse exchange,
> You that for a woman strange,
> Leave me who, with perfect love,
> Waiting you in heaven above,
> Had in my chamber richly dressed
> A bed of bliss your soul to rest?
> Terrible is your mistake!
> Unless you better council take,
> In heaven your bed shall be unmade,
> And in the flames of hell be spread."[8]

Mary behaves like any other jilted lover. Far removed is the compassionate mother whose only pleasure is the welfare of her children. She is a hurt woman here, jealous, vengeful, vulnerable. The source of her power is the love of those she loves: it is derived not from an infinite, infallible divine source, but from the hearts of those devoted to her, and any sign of slackening devotion is a potential threat to her own love-image. The refusal to relinquish love is for woman instinctual self-preservation. Love to a woman is life. Unloving and unloved she is unable to exist.

Another incident of intended infidelity by one of Mary's devotees, also recorded in an early medieval French poem, reveals a similar reaction of chagrin and vengefulness on the part of the Holy Virgin. This was the case of a young chevalier who repeatedly besought her help in his unrequited love affair. Here again, Mary the woman, not Mary the mother, responded to the supplications of the unhappy lover.

> "She who has caused you thus to sigh,
> And has brought you to this end"—
> Said Our Lady—"Tell me, friend,
> Is she handsomer than I?"
> Scared by her brilliancy, the knight
> Knows not what to do for fright;
> He clasps his hands before his face,
> And in his shame and his disgrace
> Falls prostrate on the ground with fear;
> But she with pity ever near
> Tells him: "Friend, be not afraid!
> Doubt not that I am she whose aid
> Shall surely bring your love to you;
> But take good care what you shall do!
> She you shall love most faithfully
> Of us two, shall your mistress be."[9]

Scarcely can one find in literature evidence of feminine rivalry more eloquent, or possessiveness more forcefully portrayed. These early French songs, religious and popular, convincingly establish Mary as a woman of intrigue and innocence. French literature centuries later uses the same image to portray the belle Juive.

The fact that Manette of the Goncourts was a woman of caprice; that the Jewess of Victor Hugo was a sultana of tyrannical tastes and ambitions; that Maupassant's Rachel and Raphaële[10] were indiscriminate in their choices of lovers does not in the tradition of French writing detract from their idealized image. Rather, it makes them worthy descendants of the glorified proto-mistress, virtual replicas of Mary.

In the words of Henry Adams, "Mary was as unscrupulous as any other great lady in abusing her advantages. . . . Frenchmen never found fault with abuses of power for what they thought a serious object. The more tyrannical Mary was, the more her adorers adored. . . ."[11]

Leon Daudet missed the mark when, in order to stigmatize a Jewish family as immoral, he presented the daughter of the house as a typical courtesan. The description of the young Jewess as "the girl Judith, a beautiful brunette, but without morals, savage; and her best dressed lovers were quickly abandoned at whim."[12]

Balzac gave graphic expression to that special quality of the feminine in the Jewess image which combines the mundane and the holy, the sexual and the saintly, by portraying his belle Juive in the role of the Magdalene. His Esther, the common courtesan, exhibits queenly magnificence which holds captive men who rule the world. She has the gift of intellect which can communicate mood and feeling, and respond with understanding and sympathy to the moods and feelings of others. Yet Esther, the redeemed harlot, the pious, gentle neophyte who astonishes her saintly companions in the convent with her spirituality, continues to harbor in her soul a vital drive toward the sexual, an almost savage compulsion to a physical expression of love.

As a harlot, Esther is nicknamed the Torpedo by her admirers, who express regret that she became the mistress of one man. Their conversation reveals that quality which sets the belle Juive apart:

> ". . . Lucien is living with the Torpedo."
>
> "What an irreparable loss," said Blondet, "to the world of literature, science, art and politics! The Torpedo is the one common whore with the makings of a true hetaira. . . . We should have bestowed on our time one of those magnificent Aspian figures without which no age can be great. . . . du Tillet would have bought her a town house, Lousteau a coach, Rastignac lackeys, des Lupeaulx a cook, Finot providing hats, Vernou would have advertised her, Bixiou would have supplied her witticisms! Ah, what a loss! she would have embraced a whole century, and is in love with a commonplace young man!"
>
> ". . . The Torpedo knows how to laugh and how to make others laugh. This skill of great authors and great actors belongs to those who have penetrated to the depth of society. . . . She holds a magic wand with which she unlooses the brutish appetites so violently curbed in men not without heart who are occupied in politics or science, literature or art. There is no woman in Paris who can so effectively say to the Animal: 'Out. . . .' And the Animal trots from its kennel, and it wallows in excesses. . . . In fact this woman is the salt celebrated by Rabelais which, sprinkled on matter, animates it and raises it to the wonderful realms of Art. . . ."
>
> "You have all been more or less her lovers, none of you can say she was his mistress; she can have you any time, but you won't get her. . . ."

"But what made me elect her queen is her Bourbonian indifference to the fallen favorite."[13]

The same woman, after her entrance into the convent, presents a contrasting picture. The partly mocking, partly reverent, commendation of the Torpedo's exceptional qualities in the above passage is now replaced by an awe-struck litany of her spiritual excellence:

> (Her) look cast no dread fascination but rather a gentle warmth, it weakened the hardest will by its mild heat. Esther had overcome hatred, she had astounded the rakes of Paris, and in the end that look and the sweetness of her smooth skin had bestowed upon her the dreadful nickname which already provided the inscription for her tomb. In her, everything was harmoniously in character.... The young boarders began with jealousy of her miracles of beauty, but ended in admiration. Before a week had passed they had taken simple Esther to their hearts ... who was to bring to the archbishop the glory of the conversion of a Jewess to Catholicism, to the convent the festival of her baptism. They forgave her her beauty.... These women had never in their teaching career met with a nature more amiable, a more Christian gentleness, truer modesty, nor so great a desire to learn.
>
> "She is an edification," said Mother Superior, kissing her on the forehead.
>
> This essentially Catholic word told all.[14]

While her transformation from sinner to saint seems complete, Esther's former self continues to plague her. Eventually it becomes the instrument of her doom.

> She also, without knowing it herself, was gnawed at by the love in her heart, a strange love, a desire more violent in her who knew all than it is in a virgin who knows nothing, although both desires had the same cause and the same purpose.... Was the sight of him for whom such angelic efforts were being made necessary to her whom God must forgive for mingling human with divine love? The one had led to the other.... She was outwardly suave as a virgin earth-bound only by her feminine shape, inwardly a raging Messalina.[15]

And so the belle Juive who wishes to abolish her vital sexuality by subordinating it to spirituality, which is also her inherent trait and birthright, creates an insoluble conflict within her soul. She does not realize that as courtesan she had fulfilled a role in harmony with her essential nature, and that her yearning for purity is not an alien ambition imposed upon that nature but one that flows from it. Erroneously she struggles against her basic sexuality. And when the furious battle seems finally lost, Esther destroys herself.

In the examples of the belle Juive at which we have been looking, the Christianity-Judaism conflict is absent. And so is the leitmotif of tragedy. The belle Juive, unlike most of her fictional sisters, stays alive to the end of the play or novel. The exception is Esther of Balzac. It is no coincidence that she, the only belle Juive with a religious-symbolic role, is also the only belle Juive doomed to a tragic end.

Two sensational actresses of Jewish origins, Rachel and Sarah Bernhardt, rose to prominence on the French stage, then virtually swept through European capitals in a wave of adulation inspired by their dramatic talent, electrifying appearance, and a mystique derived from their Jewishness.

Born Rachel Felix, the daughter of a poor, itinerant Jewish peddler from the ghettoes of Germany and Switzerland, Rachel radiated a "biblical" beauty. This, combined with an extraordinary dramatic force, established her as one of the world's great tragediennes. Her first success in the Comédie-Française launched her not only into stardom but into a series of love affairs with famous men. Successively, she was the mistress of Count Colonna-Wilensky, the illegitimate son of Napoleon, Alfred de Musset, Prince de Joinville, and Prince Jerome, the nephew of Napoleon. Her well-publicized romances, her spectacular fame as an international celebrity, and her widely admired dark, dramatic beauty undoubtedly contributed to the creation of the fabulous belle Juive.

The "divine" Sarah Bernhardt, although baptized during her adolescence, was generally identified as a Jewess, perhaps because of the "Jewess" Rachel who preceded her in that role. At the height of the Dreyfus affair, for instance, anti-Semitic mobs surrounded her carriage and shouted anti-Semitic denunciations, calling the passionately patriotic grande dame of the French theatre a traitor. Sarah Bernhardt's appeal as an actress of great emotional depth, sensitivity, and passion, her beauty and fiery temperament and courage correspond to the qualifications of the belle Juive.

An American contemporary rivalled Rachel and Sarah Bernhardt in dark, striking beauty and fascinating personality. She was the flamboyant Jewish Southern belle, Adah Isaacs Menken. An exciting actress and talented poet, the unpredictable Adah remained an enigma to her friends, and their number was legion. It included Walt Whitman, Bret Harte, Mark Twain, Longfellow, Joaquin Miller, Charles Dickens, Charles Reade, D. G. Rossetti, Théophile Gautier, Burne-Jones, George Sand, and Thomas Buchanan Reade. President Lincoln invited her to lunch at the White House. Both Alexandre Dumas (père) and Algernon Swinburne claimed she had been their mistress. The latter articulated the adoration of many in his poem "Dolores":

> Thou wert fair in the fearless old fashion
> And thy limbs are as melodies yet,
> And move to the music of passion
> With lithe and lascivious regret.
> What ailed us, O gods, to desert you
> For creeds that refuse and restrain?
> Come down and redeem us from virtue,
> Our Lady of Pain.[16]

At the height of her career, in the midst of acclaim in London and Paris where admirers flocked about her, the fiery actress collapsed during a rehearsal in 1868. The event created a sensation in the French capital and, during the final months of her short life, the beautiful Jewess was a major topic of general interest. She was "the world's delight" according to Swinburne; and Joaquin Miller recalled: "Books, a shelf-load of books, could not hold the half that has been written of this Jewish woman's beauty of form; but to me her fascination lay in her beauty of mind; her soul and sweet sympathy, her sensibility to all that was beautiful in form, colors, action, life, heart, humanity." E. C. Mayne, in his *Enchanters of Men,* included Adah Isaacs Menken among the most remarkable sirens of all time.[17] A perfect model for the belle Juive figure, Adah, at the center of Paris society and its limelight, did probably even more to fertilize French literature with the image of the fabulous Jewish courtesan than the French idols. Her "lofty" soul within an enticing body, her sudden, tragic death—are these not reminiscent of Balzac's Esther?

The most "romantic" of Jewesses served as springboard for the more complex belle Juive of the next era. Still basically the sensual woman, this new Jewish heroine is a product of momentous historical developments that exercised an irreversible impact on Jewish destiny—Jewry is polarized in its response—a fierce new sense of Jewish identity is born on the one hand, and a desperate drive toward assimilation appears on the other. The sultry, magnetic Jewess becomes the symbol of both trends.

6

Zionism versus Assimilation

> She was not less beautiful when, sitting on the camp-stool, or leaning on the deck, her face turned toward the shores of Judea, she appeared to be immersed in her thoughts. Her eyelids, almost always lowered, were not raised in these moments of repose, her glance was as if veiled by a passionate preoccupation; it has been rumored that she retains a flame for some mysterious contemplation. Her magic charm was most intense upon those who observed her then, and indeed when she arose after her silent raptures and turned her eyes about her, the boat became as if illuminated. . . . all glances clung to her and followed all her movements.[1]

The precursor of the modern Zionist Jewess in French literature is Rebecca of Mme. Rattazzi's *La Belle Juive* (1882). An intensely beautiful young woman, Rebecca sublimates her sexuality into a fierce passion for Zion. She is on her way to Palestine at a time when few undertook such an enterprise. It was the beginning of what we now call the First Aliyah—the first wave of modern history's Jewish emigration to Zion. That first wave consisted of a small group of young men and women, mostly university students from Russia. At the time it was an obscure, modest venture. In retrospect, it was the beginning of Modern Israel. The first Aliyah laid the foundations of the Jewish State. The visionary Jewess, setting forth on a pilgrimage to Judea driven by Zionist zeal, must be considered a prototype of the modern

Jew, a forerunner of a string of similar figures to appear during the twentieth century.

Her frame of reference as sexual as ever, the Zionist Jewess is erotically present even in her detachment from her surroundings. Although her soul is in Zion, her physical being continues to create excitement:

> He met the glance of the woman. That profound yet untamed glance, having passed through a double civilization, antique and modern, was it more caressing or more threatening? It had a long thrill of sensuality and dread. The beautiful eyes reflected I know not how many vast conquests—all the victorious Orient during hundred centuries regenerated, amid young nations, in the lascivious and scorching skin of Israel.[2]

The emancipation of the Jews of France brought about drastic changes in their status during the nineteenth century. Their rise from economic plight to financial and industrial success, from oppression and obscurity to social prominence was phenomenal. Playing an important role in French commerce and industry, the Jew within half a century came to occupy prominent positions also in intellectual and political life. Soon Jewish influence was felt in art, music, and scholarship. By the end of the century, the entry of the Jew into the mainstream of French life and his eager assimilation into French culture often culminated in his conversion to Christianity. Finally he felt he belonged.

He did not, and soon found out. During the last decade of the century, the Jews of France were confronted with demonstrations of anti-Jewish hostility on a scale frightening not only to them but to liberal observers the world over. It was an eruption of latent resentment that had been rising since mid-century. In literature there had been startlingly prolific outpourings of anti-Semitism, with an array of new Jew villains appearing in every new publication. As in Germany, so now in France the earlier Jew villain of minor importance was transformed into an ominous figure—the powerful international banker, unethical financier, or parvenu capitalist. Balzac, Zola, Bonnières and others seemed to outdo each other in portraying the unscrupulous Jew out to get Christian society. Others dealt with "Jewish opportunism" in turning baptism to financial or political gain, exploiting Christian honesty and naiveté in devious ways.

The Jewess image acquired new dimensions. By reaction or contrast, perhaps, the unscrupulousness of the Jewish male seems to have rendered her even more sensitive to ethical values, even more high-principled than her predecessors. Vulnerable to the tide of events and ideologies, the literary Jewess figure nevertheless serves as ethical yardstock against which to measure society.

The rise of anti-Semitism prompted two main reactions among the Jews. Out of one reaction, political Zionism was born. In a dramatic sense, it was born on the streets of Paris during the mass demonstrations against Dreyfus and Jews—in the trauma of a disillusioned assimilationist. He was Dr. Theodor Herzl, a Viennese journalist and popular playwright sent to Paris by the *Allgemeiner Zeitung* to cover the Dreyfus trial. In the outpouring of mob hate against Jews on the streets of civilized Paris, Herzl saw the writing on the wall for European Jewry. His solution: a Jewish homeland. The method of achieving it was clearly to organize support and to obtain an internationally guaranteed charter for such a state.

Herzl's passion for the idea flamed into missionary zeal and in time fired the imagination of many others. The cry for a Jewish homeland became international. It gained adherents even among Jews who a few years earlier had been staunch proponents of assimilation. Bitter now about its failure, Jews responded to the call of political Zionism, as it came to be known—the planned exodus of Jews from a Christian Europe which continued to reject them.

The second reaction was its polar opposite. Many Jews felt that assimilation had not worked because it had not been wholehearted enough; now they threw themselves into an even more passionate drive for "Europeanism." Baptism and intermarriage were the avowed objectives of many in this group, and their convictions endured until the last death train carried some of the most devout converts to Auschwitz.

The fictional Jewess of the era mirrors both trends. She is either a Zionist enamoured of Zion, the ancient Jewish homeland, or a convert to Christianity. But, unlike her father who converts for ulterior motives, the Jewess does so out of conviction.

In either case, the Christian-Jewess relationship suffers. The Zionist Jewess, classically the representative of prophetic Judaism, now becomes a visionary of the Zionist dream. The conflict she feels in her love for a Christian becomes more acute. The differences seem irreconcilable. The devout convert, on the other hand, deplores matrimony for money—hers. She recoils from the union, preferring the loss of love to the loss of personal dignity. She is once again, both as woman and as Jewess, victimized by male ambitions—her lover's greed for money and her father's greed for social advancement.

Both Jewesses are amply evident in the literature of the age. Enacryos's Rachel, in *La Juive* the woman with "that profound yet untamed glance," belongs to the first group: she is an ardent Zionist. One of the period's Jewish millionaires falls in love with this girl of meager finances but dazzling beauty. She accepts his offer of marriage although she does not love him, and for a while lives apparently contented by the luxury and security that surround her.

Her husband's sudden death awakens Rachel, both as Jewess and as woman. Coming into contact with Zionism, her sense of Jewish identity is born, and she plunges into zealous activity for the Zionist cause. Simultaneously, she meets a Christian man with whom she falls passionately in love. Contradictory as this may seem, the diehard Zionist can find no Jew to arouse her passion. Stranger yet, the man who does is an anti-Semite.

The two conflicting drives in her intense personality make the relationship with Varades, her lover, a stormy affair. While Rachel is propagating Jewish national aspirations in order to ensure Jewry's survival, Varades argues for the assimilation of Jewry into European culture in order to annihilate it. Rachel loves Judaism. Varades despises it.

At first, Rachel's womanly passion overrides her Jewish passion. She changes, however, when an anti-Semite shoots and kills her father-in-law, in whose house she has been living since the death of her husband. Unable to continue her love affair with the anti-Semite Varades, she retreats into a total commitment to Zionist work. Though she finds a new lover, a Zionist, he is not capable of arousing her passion as the anti-Semite did. Just as well, for now Rachel is free to devote her entire being to the Zionist cause.

Several French Christian authors exhibited a remarkable interest in Zionist aspirations. Ever since Napoleon's proclamation during his Egyptian campaign in 1798–99 that he would favor "the restoration of Jerusalem to its ancient glory," Frenchmen have harbored a fascination for the Zionist idea. In 1860 the private secretary of Napoleon III, Ernest Laharanne, a Roman Catholic, published a pamphlet entitled "Reestablishment of Jewish Nationality," in which he appealed to France to help Jews realize their dream of a homeland in Palestine "under the aegis of France, the Emancipator." Nobel Peace Prize winner, humanitarian and founder of the International Red Cross, Henri Dunant was also a Christian advocate of Jewish settlement in Palestine. In 1863 he appealed to Jews for their support of a colonization committee he had set up in Paris under the patronage of Empress Eugénie. Léon Bourgeois, Prime Minister of France (1895–96), wrote that "anti-Semitism is opposed to culture," and in order to "bring relief to a persecuted and unfortunate people" a Jewish Homeland must be established in Palestine. Such a homeland for Jews, "a nation newly reconstituted, full of energy and composed of such intelligent, capable and talented elements," would naturally bring about "an increase in the general work of culture."[3]

The early Zionist ideologues and leaders took these pronouncements seriously, and saw in France a practical ally. Moses Hess, a forerunner of Zionist thought, in his major work *Rome and Jerusalem* (1862), wrote: "Do you still doubt that France will help the Jews to found colonies which may extend from Suez to Jerusalem and from the banks of the Jordan to the coast of the Mediterranean? . . . France will extend the work of redemption also to the Jewish nation . . . Frenchmen and Jews! It seems that in all things they were created for one another." Half a century later, when political Zionism had become an organized reality, one of its world leaders, Max Nordau, indicated to French statesmen that he favored French influence in Constantinople on behalf of Jews and even a French protectorate over Palestine. He advocated that political Zionism should seek only the support of France because, he felt, the Jewish mentality was akin to the French spirit.[4]

Ironically the same period produced some of the most virulent anti-Semitic writing in France. Anti-Semitic agitation cynically exploited even Zionist aspirations. The idea of establishing a homeland for Jews in Palestine and having them emigrate there sounded like an ideal solution to those who resented the Jews' presence in France, Germany, or anywhere else in Europe. Several anti-Semitic authors of the period utilized their writing to promote pro-Zionist sentiments.

Maurice Donnay, for example, in his play *Le Retour de Jerusalem* (1903), espoused Zionism and anti-Semitism simultaneously. He chose the figure of a Jewess to accomplish both in one. Judith, the product of an assimilationist background, is the daughter of a nouveau riche Jewish banker. Possessing an extraordinary physical appeal, a brilliant mind, and versatile talents, Judith is well-read, speaks several languages, and plays several musical instruments; she has passed more than one scholastic examination with distinction and holds multiple university degrees.

At the Sorbonne Judith meets her Christian, the handsome Count de Chouzé. He falls in love with the extraordinary Jewess, and she in love with him. In order to marry him, she converts to Christianity. Nevertheless, the new Countess de Chouzé is not happy. She realizes that her conversion has not made her a Christian. She feels that she has remained a Jewess despite baptism, despite change of name and social rank. In the Gentile milieu her Jewish identity is acutely brought home to her. True to herself, Judith leaves her Christian home and husband, takes back her former name and returns to Judaism.

A new vista opens for Judith. Awareness of her Jewish identity gives new direction to her life. She becomes a Zionist. She dreams of visiting the Promised Land of her forefathers. She yearns to do penance at the Wailing Wall in Jerusalem for the sin of having converted to Christianity. Only then, she believes, will her return to Judaism be complete.

Judith falls in love again—again with a Christian! Michel is a married man, but he is so hopelessly in love with the irresistible Jewess that he leaves his wife. This time, however, Judith enters the relationship on her own terms. She does not compromise her Jewishness: it is the Christian lover who offers to submerge himself in her identity. He even agrees to join her on her journey to Jerusalem. Together they make the pilgrimage of her dreams to the Wailing Wall. Together they pray there for the Jewish people and for their joint future.

Despite all of Michel's goodwill, the Jewish-Christian harmony does not last. Back in Paris, they set up a household frequented only by Judith's Jewish friends, vulgar, aggressive, unscrupulous characters. Michel's latent dislike of Jews turns to open hatred. He spouts the anti-Semitic generalities in vogue at the time. They quarrel and break up. Michel leaves Judith to the company of her decadent Jewish friends and returns to his wife.

In this plot the liaisons fall apart not because convention looks askance at Jewish-Christian relationships but because of the unassimilability of the Jewish psyche. Jews will be Jews, says Donnay, no matter how intelligent, no matter how talented they are, and no matter how hard a Christian might try to accommodate them. There is no compromise with Jews, there is no integration with them. Each should seek his own.

Interestingly, Michel's anti-Semitism remains latent during his trip to Palestine. He even reconciles himself to wailing among the Jews at the Wailing Wall. The uncultured sounds, sights, and smells of nineteenth-century east Jerusalem are agreeable enough to his French sensibilities. It is only the society of Jews in Paris which offends his taste and makes him turn against Jews in general.

Donnay's "Zionism" is in effect based on racist anti-Semitism. The view of the Jew as a race, rather than a religion, made its appearance in the second half of the century. The anti-clerical trend of republican France would have perhaps eliminated anti-Semitism as a weapon if such prejudices were promulgated entirely on religious grounds. Nor could the fierce patriotism of conservatives have isolated the Jew who often outdid them in chauvinism. But the allegation that the Jew was racially different, that the stereotypical negative traits of the Jew were genetically integral to his personality was an irrefutable argument. It could, and did, appeal to both camps, and the Jews were powerless to defend themselves against it.

If racial, then the traits of aggressiveness, greed, vulgarity, etc., were unchangeable, and therefore there was no hope in assimilating the Jew through education or social reforms. The only solution lay in isolating him. And what better method of isolation could be devised than creating a homeland for the lot, a homeland at a safe distance from the shores of Europe, and shipping them there en masse? This proposal reminds one of Adolf Eichmann's Madagascar Plan.

The French anti-Semitic writings of this period did indeed serve as a basis for Nazi ideology and propaganda. Donnay calls the Christian hero "Aryan," and the Jewish heroine "Asian." The works of Toussenel, Proudhon, Drumont, Daudet, and Céline served as inspiration to Nazi ideologues of the twentieth century. The novels of Léon Daudet and Ferdinand Céline were translated into German by the official Nazi propaganda machine for use as educational material in the Nazi state.

How did the Jews of France respond to Zionist taunts by anti-Semitic writers? Those with Zionist aspirations treated them as they would any other anti-Semitic declarations—as proof positive of a need for Zionist aspirations. Those with assimilationist zeal—by repudiating Zionism and dissociating themselves from it with even greater vehemence.

The classic stereotype of the medieval Jew was not a threat to an assimilated Jew, but when the modern Jew was portrayed as nonetheless "typically Jewish," especially when this was not done for obviously anti-Semitic ends, it constituted a threat to his identity as a Frenchman. Reference to Zionism caused true consternation among Jews who wished to be considered Frenchmen, first and foremost.

Alaxandre Dumas' *La Femme de Claude* (1873) was one of the first Zionist plays by a Christian to create fear and furor among French Jews. Though a positive portrayal of Jews, its disturbing feature for proponents of assimilation is the passionately "Jewish" tendency of the characters. The protagonist, Daniel, is an extraordinary human being with the finest human traits and patriotic loyalties. But this paragon of virtue is a visionary consumed by his fervor for a Jewish future in Zion. In the opinion of the liberal Catholic historian Anatole Leroy-Beaulieu, Daniel is superior to Lessing's famous Nathan in the epoch-making eighteenth-century drama *Nathan the Wise.* "Lessing," he states, "is not the only author who dares to show us a Jew upon a pedestal of virtue. To his Nathan the Wise, the virtuous logician, surrounded by a chilly halo of wisdom, I prefer Daniel of *La Femme de Claude,* a Jew who is much more idealistic than the Paris jackanapes would have thought a Jew to be."[5] Jewish audiences, with minor exception, rejected the authenticity of the Daniel figure and were aghast at the ideas he propounded. Did they prefer the stereotypical Jew villain to a Zionist hero? Was their failure to object to Shylock, and their outrage at Daniel, an indication that they considered Shylock the more authentic Jew? Had Jewish self-hatred reached such a low point in the late nineteenth century, the so-called pre-Nazi period?

The contemporary Jewish drama critic, Abraham Dreyfus, who had found no objection to the unfavorable portrayal of Jews on stage, considering it merely an old literary habit, viewed with alarm Dumas' portrayal. He bitterly ridiculed Dumas for turning Daniel and his daughter into veritable angels preaching the return of Jews to the Promised Land. In his study "Le Juif au Théâtre" he wrote with considerable scorn: "Thirteen years ago, when he first produced *La Femme de Claude*, the noted writer wanted to send us off to Palestine. . . . But it appears that, appealing though they were, Daniel and Rebecca did not succeed in winning over most of the Jews who were firmly established in Paris." Dreyfus speaks for the majority of French Jewish audiences when he insists that "For these Jews there is only one Fatherland, which has adopted them and which they love and defend."[6]

Although the Zionist aspect of the play attracted the most attention because of its potential for controversy, Dumas' main objective as moralist was to preach patriotism and family purity. He chose the Jewess as the vehicle for his moral message. It was through the figure of the Jewess that all the sacred ideals of the age—to honor God, country, work, marriage, and motherhood—were represented on the Paris stage. His drama reflected an upsurge of conservative values as a reaction to the Franco-Prussian War of 1871. In his prologue Dumas asserted that Corneille's *Le Cid,* although a great work of art, did not have moral significance. The heroine, Chimène, in her great love for Rodrigo should have given him up instead of marrying him. A woman should be led by virtue, said Dumas, rather than the pursuit of personal happiness.

Rebecca the Jewess is such a woman of virtue. Her Cid is Claude, a French Christian married to a woman who is Rebecca's antithesis.

He loves the remarkably beautiful and kind Jewess and, in order to spend his life in the bliss of that love, he wishes to dissolve his marriage. Rebecca requites his love with equal passion, but to her the sanctity of marriage is supreme, and she sacrifices her love on its altar. "She sacrifices herself," explains the playwright through one of his characters, "in her youth, in her beauty."

Rebecca is the mouthpiece of Dumas, the ethical prophet. She herself is cast in the role of prophet, proclaiming to humanity that there is a realm of supernatural morality where man's petty concerns shrink into insignificance. In her farewell to Claude she expresses a spiritual view of existence, a mystical concept of love.

> When death shall have freed us, you from the bonds, me from terrestial submissions, you will find me, a patient and unmaterial bride, awaiting you on the threshold of the unknown and we shall be united in the Infinite. . . . I am the bride of the second life.[7]

Rebecca is the perfect woman, a saint. She is often more saint than human, an ideal specimen for the pedestal, and a fitting addition to the collection of classic Jewess types in literature.

Despite Dreyfus's claim, there were French Jews who responded positively to the Zionist idea. Lazar Levy-Bing, a banker and member of the French National Assembly, maintained that there was no conflict between aspirations for a Jewish homeland in Palestine and Jewish loyalty to France. The *Alliance Israelite Universelle,* founded in 1860 to help Jews the world over, extended its assistance to educational institutions in Palestine. Young students in Paris began to group together and form Zionist associations. As early as 1881 they founded an organization in Paris called "Eternal Jew" which spread to other towns. The controversy between assimilation and Zionism, between French patriotism and Jewish identity, became more heated as anti-Semitism grew into a political weapon and Zionism into a political force. During the last decade of the century, the various World Zionist Congresses attracted the attention of an increasing number of Jews and resulted in an ever-widening, if mostly ideological, sphere of influence. The Zionist now felt his ideas vindicated, his dream not altogether insane; the assimilationist felt called upon to prove with dramatic gestures his French loyalties. French Jews turned to the Church in impressive numbers and celebrated their conversion to Christianity with lavish parties attended by Christian well-wishers. It was the choice to make if you believed in the ideas of the Revolution, and if you truly loved your fatherland.

French literature also reflects these responses and their implications. Once again, through the agency of the Jewish heroine, a whole gamut of issues is articulated. How does such a drastic step as conversion affect a Jew, even if he is an assimilated Jew? How does it affect his future? The Jewess supposedly is more sensitive, more vulnerable, more complex, than other people. Her reactions are therefore a more precise barometer of the emotional and mental world under scrutiny. Although she is on a pedestal, she is a product of her world, or of the way the author perceives it.

Some twenty years after the first production of Dumas' play and the appearance of the Rebecca role on the Paris stage, Paul Bourget presented a similarly remarkable, saintly beauty in his novel *Cosmopolis* (1892). She is Fanny Hafner, the daughter of a parvenu Jewish banker. A "typical" Jew, Hafner is not concerned with ethics or ideals, to him religion is a matter of convenience. Or inconvenience. The only true religion in the Hafner household is money: it is money they worship; it is money that gives meaning to their lives.

Fanny is different. She is unhappy in such a home. She grows up with a hunger for spiritual meaning. Her need remains unfulfilled until after the death of her mother, when she meets a simple Catholic woman who takes her under her wing and provides the spiritual enlightenment that the Jewish home failed to do. For the first time in her life, the lovely Jewess finds true happiness. With childlike devotion she clings to her new friend, and her new faith. In her religious zeal she becomes inseparable from her mentor who was

> . . . obviously inferior, a provincial lady in charge of serving as chaperon for the other, a young girl of near sublime beauty with large black eyes burning in a pale complexion, a pallor warm and alive. Her profile of Oriental purity embodied too completely the typical Jewish beauty to leave any doubt as to the Hebrew origin of this creature, a genuine phenomenon which seemed compelled to, as the poet said, "draw all hearts behind her!"
>
> And I am quite certain that Helen [of Troy] did not have such modern gracefulness, such feeling in her beauty, such an ideal profile, such a profound glance, such a dreamy mouth and such a smile. . . . Ah, how beautiful she is![8]

Fanny, "the typical Jewish beauty," believes that after death her place in heaven is assured once the Church receives her in its bosom. She marries a Catholic and expects bliss to follow. However, in earthly existence happiness eludes her. The marriage does not work. Fanny, like a true Jewess (or Christian) bears her suffering stoically, praying for life everlasting to redeem her. Only in heaven will her search end.

The isolation of the uprooted Jew in search of identity and roots is dramatically illustrated in the figure of Fanny Hafner. While Bourget's male Jews are depicted as unredeemable villains beyond the scope of reader sympathy, the Jewish heroine presents the human element in the Jewish dilemma. Fanny Hafner is the vulnerable Jew exposed to the whim of social forces in turn-of-century France, just as Abigail had been in sixteenth-century England. While the interplay of forces had changed, the basic issue is still the same—the Jew versus the Christian world.

Bourget's Fanny Hafner was preceded by a fictional Jewish heroine whose portrayal of conflict is even more poignant. She is Lia Monach in Robert de Bonnières' novel *Les Monachs* (1885). This book is a fierce diatribe against assimilated Jews in which, once again, it is up to the Jewess to serve as a counterpoint to the rabid hostility of the Jewish male characters. Once again it is up to her to articulate the human drama of Jewish reality.

Lia Monach is stereotypically beautiful, captivating, pious, intelligent, sensitive, and selfless. From her pious grandmother, the sensitive young girl absorbs a profound love of Judaism, but her father, an opportunistic Jewish huckster, wants her to be a success in the Gentile world and weans her away from Jewish influences. Lia is bewildered by the ambivalence of her environment and grows up searching for approval among her Christian classmates. In Christian society, however, she is greeted with hostility. Her beauty and wealth are envied, her company is resented. Lia the outsider devotes her adult life to becoming an insider. Finally she makes her way into a segment of French society which superficially admires wealth and the power inherent in it.

The intelligent, sensitive Lia knows her acceptance is not genuine. She determines to become a Christian, hoping that membership in the Church will gain her membership in Gentile society. She might have imagined herself successful in this, had she not become engaged to Roger, the son of a French general. They are about to marry when Lia discovers that Roger is marrying her for her money. The news crushes Lia's carefully constructed self-image; she breaks off the engagement. Roger's entreaties of love, by now genuine, do not help. The traumatized Jewess retreats into a world of seclusion. In vain her father attempts to console her. In vain he attempts to cajole her into meeting other eligible young Christians. She spurns every proposal of marriage.

Savoir and Nozière presented a carbon copy of Lia in their anti-Semitic comedy *Le Baptême* staged in 1907 in Paris. The daughter of

German Jews grown rich in France, Hélène Bloch is as lovely, charming, and impressionable as Lia Monach. She, too, reaches the emotional stage of "growth" where baptism becomes inevitable. For her, too, conversion to Christianity is the sole avenue of emotional and social adjustment. She is overwhelmed with the new social milieu that now opens before her. Among the visitors at the newly-converted, nouveau riche Jewish household is the bishop himself, in the company of young Count de Croissy.

The young Christian becomes Hélène's suitor. Acting as patron and matchmaker, the bishop arranges a match between the Jewess and the count. At first Hélène is dazzled by her apparent good fortune. But when she finds out that the count's single object is her dowry, she is deeply shocked. In her pain she resolves never to marry but to become a nun at Lourdes.

Ironically, the convent refuses to accept her without a substantial monetary contribution. At first her rejection seems final, for her "typical" Jewish father refuses to cooperate; but when the financial and social advantages of such a contribution are pointed out to him by his clever wife, the miserly Jew relents. His resignation to the loss of ducats and daughter parallels Shylock's. In fact, Monsieur Bloch is Shylock. And while Bloch-Shylock is the intended butt of the anti-Semitic farce, it is Hélène who is the ultimate victim.

The theme reiterates the notion that conversion to Christianity does not solve the Jewish problem. No matter how hard he tries, the Jew cannot undo his Jewishness. It works neither from the Christian nor from the Jewish point of view: baptism does not render the Jew less odious to Christian eyes, neither does it provide him with instant identity.

In the nineteenth century both the Christian and the Jew considered Judaism an unalienable legacy. Judaism was thought to be more than a religion, more than a culture; it was rather like a genetic-mystic bond. Pseudo-scientists spoke of a "Jewish race." This new definition of Jewishness became the rationale for the new flare-up of anti-Semitism: racist-nationalist anti-Semitism now replaced the earlier religion-oriented prejudice. Anti-Semites who exploited the "scientific" theory of Jewry as race claimed that it was unredeemable by baptism. Those anti-Semites who insisted that Judaism was a nationality concentrated their campaign on this aspect of the definition and declared the Jews aliens in the lands of their birth. In an age of extreme chauvinism and idealization of "roots," this argument likewise rendered both baptism and assimilation futile. It rendered the Jews' political emancipation futile. Bitterly, the Jews discovered that citizenship did not mean national identity. Having been born in a country for generations, having adopted language, customs, culture, having given love, loyalty, and service to a fatherland did not make the Jew an integral part.

In England George Eliot in *Daniel Deronda* (1876) depicts the Jew caught up in futile efforts at assimilation and denial of Jewish identity. The Jewish dilemma is presented here through the figure of Mme. Alcharisi, a Spanish Jewish singer who deludes herself into believing that masking Jewishness will actually create a new identity. She is determined to provide her infant son, Daniel, with a chance to break totally with his Jewish ancestry. To bring him up in ignorance of his background, she gives the boy to an aristocratic British admirer for adoption. Sir Hugo Mallinger is true to his pledge, and Daniel Deronda grows up unaware of his Jewish "race."

The cherished hope of Madame Alcharisi is disappointed, however. The ruse does not work. Even before he is recognized by a banker friend of his grandfather, Daniel senses that he is different. He behaves "like a Jew": he is kind to his fellows and offers assistance to the poor. By coincidence he makes contact with Jews and singles them out as targets of his kindness and generosity.

Through a chance meeting with his grandfather's friend, Daniel meets his mother, and to his delight and the latter's dismay finds out about his parentage. Madame Alcharisi finds little comfort in her son's pride in being a Jew. She has no choice but reluctantly to face the fact: a Jew may never divest himself of his Jewishness. Like predestination in Greek thought, Jewishness, if genetically inherited, is inescapable.

Almost twenty years later another English novelist chose to treat the theme of Jewish identity crisis through the figure of a Jewess. Like Eliot's, Walter Besant's protagonist in *The Rebel Queen* (1893), Mme. Elveda, is also a Spanish Jewess bent on concealing her Jewish identity and that of her daughter. Her helpless fury against the yoke of Jewish legacy is revealed in the hostility she feels toward members of her own family:

> "I renounce the people," said she to her husband, "I belong to them no longer. Your old traditions, your jumble, and jargon of ceremonies and superstitions, I will follow no longer. I throw them off."

Her husband, Emanuel Elveda, a man of intellect and national pride, knows that a Jew cannot "throw off" his identity:

> "You cannot renounce your people," said he with conviction. "Any other man or woman may renounce his race and enter another

nation; you cannot. None of us may renounce our people. On our faces there is a mark set—the seal of the Lord, by which we know each other and are known by the world."[9]

Madame Elveda, like Madame Alcharisi, is a deviation from the Jewess stereotype. She is not the young, innocent daughter of the Jew: she is the experienced, mature woman of the world who, keenly aware of her victimization, attempts to defeat it. Ironically, she too becomes a victim—of her struggle's ultimate futility. Even in her appearance she is the "untypical" Jewess:

> This girl was not possessed of the almond eyes, black, long, soft, and languishing, which poets used to associate with the East; she could not be painted as Leila, or as the favorite of the Harem, or anything of that kind; nor was her complexion olive; nor had she a mass of black hair. On the contrary, her eyes were brown, clear and cold and keen; tonight there was no languishing in them and no tenderness; her features were finely, clearly cut, the curve of her lips well-defined, her mouth full, firm—even hard—her nose somewhat aquiline, her forehead more square than seems to some consistent with perfect beauty; her hair brown, abundant, was rolled up and round her head confined by ribbon or band in which gleamed gold coins. . . .[10]

The stereotyped Jewess image is retained for her daughter. Young Francesca is unmistakably a Jewess. Brought up by her mother to believe she is a "Spanish Moor," Francesca is told at every turn that she looks Jewish. No denials on her part help: all her friends insist that she is a Jew. There is a whole range of qualifications which places her in that category. Finally, Madame Elveda's rebellion against Judaism and her elaborate attempt to spare her daughter the consequences of Jewish origins backfire. Francesca discovers that she is a Jewess and the news makes her just as happy and proud as it does Eliot's Daniel Deronda. Madame Elveda, on the other hand, is as bitter about the failure of her scheme as is Madame Alcharisi.

The names and descriptions of these Jewish heroines suggest that both authors modelled them after Spanish Jewish women. This was, in fact, the case with most British fiction. The fame of several Marrano women accounted for this. In addition to the figures of Maria Nuñez Pereyra and others mentioned earlier, the spectacular personality of Gracia Mendez made international news. She was the most remarkable Jewish woman of the Renaissance period. Born and married in Portugal, Gracia Nasi Mendez after the early death of her husband became the head of his banking firm and turned it into a financial empire with dealings in every European city. She led her extended family from Portugal to the Netherlands in search of religious freedom, and from there she conducted her commercial affairs with the German states, France, and Naples. Although under the protection of Queen Maria, she moved from Holland to Venice where she established a prominent name for herself as a patroness of the arts. Her extraordinary beauty and brilliance gained her both friends and foes. When on some calumny she was imprisoned by the Venetian authorities, her powerful friends intervened. Both the Sultan of Turkey and the Duke of Este invited her to settle in their countries. After her release from prison Gracia settled in Ferrara; later transferred her holdings to Constantinople. There she and her family returned to Judaism.

Both Eliot's and Besant's treatment of the Jewess is extraordinary. Their Jewesses are "liberated" women, who are treated as real people grappling with real issues. Even more remarkable, both authors arrive at a "Jewish" solution to the Christian-Jewess dilemma. In each novel the young protagonist discovers his or her Jewishness, and this brings about the happy ending: each may now marry his or her love. In earlier novels the opposite was the case: the discovery of a Christian identity produced the happy ending.

Although from the point of view of the protagonists—Madames Alcharisi and Elveda—the ending is far from satisfactory, nowhere does this even come close to the harsh fate most other Christian writers meted out to their Jewish heroines.

The dilemma of Jewess-Christian, of Jewishness versus assimilation, superimposed on the realities of Jewish life in Russia produces a somewhat starker drama. Chirikov, in his play *The Jews* (1904), presents the problem and its inevitable, tragic solution, through the figure of young Leah. Leah, the daughter of a small shopkeeper in a *shtetl* of czarist Russia, falls in love with Berezin, a young Socialist from the other end of town. The two young people attend university together, dream the Socialist dream together. Her romance with a Christian and involvement in Socialist activities bring Leah's concerns into sharp focus: she must leave the ghetto. She no longer wants to associate with the Jewish condition, with Jewish sensitivities, with Jewish fate.

Leizer, the Jewish father, explains, then argues, then pleads. But Leah is adamant. She wants the light of the outside world instead of the darkness of the ghetto. She wants to be free of the shackles of the Jewish past. A future away from the ghetto is happiness and fulfilment. Berezin and the Socialist idea are the future. After stormy debates, Leah takes the fateful step towards that future.

With Berezin, Leah moves from her Jewish home to the Christian quarter. Shortly after, there is a pogrom in the ghetto. Leah is in town with Berezin when the news reaches them. Berezin thanks God she is safe, that she left in time. He advises Leah to go with him, to hide in safety at his house until the rioting is over.

Leah does not share Berezin's relief at her safety. She does not hasten to Berezin's house. Suddenly, she knows what she must do: go back to the ghetto, where she belongs. Ignoring Berezin's pleas, she runs off.

Reaching home, Leah finds her brother murdered and her father dying of his wounds. A band of Russian peasants looting the house corners her. She manages to elude them, reach her bedroom, and there commit suicide. The murderous mob follows, breaks down the door during Leah's last moments, and amid wild laughter rape the dying Jewess.

The Socialist ferment and the Kishinev pogrom of 1903 served as background for the play. Jewish youth, caught up in the struggle for identity within the ghetto, joined the Socialist Revolution in disproportionately large numbers. The assimilationist trend from the West had reached eastern Europe during the last decades of the nineteenth century and was making inroads into the strongly traditional character of the Jewish communities in Poland and Russia. The Socialist Revolution helped precipitate the problem. The confrontation between parents adhering to tradition and children opting for "progress" was much more sharply drawn than the similar struggle between young and old Jew in the West. Whether "progress" meant Socialism or secularization, the issue was practically the same. The issue was Judaism versus assimilation, the ghetto versus the Gentile world.

In all works dealing with the conflict of Judaism versus assimilation, it was the role of the Jewess to function as Jewry's representative. As a symbol of Jewry at the core of the conflict, the Jewess emerges as liberated woman. Although exposed to and greatly affected by the powerful currents of political and social forces, she does not become their casualty. Unlike those around her, she does not fall or falter. Although often victimized, she is ultimately victor, morally triumphant whether her choice is Zionism or assimilation. The Jewish heroine is often the sole spokesman of morality, ethics, or patriotism in a decadent, corrupt society. Whether a committed Zionist or a dedicated convert to Christianity, she breaks the impasse of the Christian-Jew dilemma simply by affirming her choice. Unlike earlier Jewesses who clung to romance until rejected by their Christian lover, the liberated woman has the self-awareness and courage to reject a relationship if it lacks merit. She is no longer a sexual slave; she sees herself as an equal.

The Zionist Jewess rejects her relationship with the Christian because of irreconcilable differences. Enacryos's Rachel and Donnay's Judith find the strength to leave their anti-Semitic lovers, just as Dumas' Rebecca had relied on her moral resources to terminate her affair with the married Claude. The assimilated Jewess likewise chooses principle over ambition. Bonnières' Lia and Savoir *et* Nozière's Hélène reject marriages of convenience and sham social arrangements; they opt for the negation of all ambition. And Chirikov's Leah, when the chips are down, opts for Jewish identity. She, too, makes a choice, although she knows that this choice means personal catastrophe.

But then this was the first decade of the twentieth century when the valiant stand of morality symbolized by the Jewess was drowned in the waves of violence that were to become the century's distinguishing feature. The bloody pogroms in Russia were only the beginning. Society's silent acceptance of ever increasing brutality, the ever increasing toleration of violence, was a disturbing symptom. It was the prelude to the Holocaust.

7

Prelude to the Holocaust

"Are you Ukrainian?"
She hesitated a moment, then firmly replied: "No."
"A Jewess?"
"Yes. But how did you know? Do I talk like one?"
"No."
"Then how did you guess I was a Jewess?"
He reduced the length of his stride in an attempt to fall into step with her, and answered:
"Your ear—the shape of your ears, and your eyes.
Otherwise you show little sign of your nationality." He thought for a moment, then added: "It is good that you are with us."
"Why?" she asked inquisitively.
"Well, the Jews have a certain reputation. And I know that many workers believe it to be true—you see I am a worker, too—that the Jews do all the ordering and don't go under fire themselves. That is not true, and you do prove splendidly that it isn't true."[1]

Anna is a fervent Bolshevik, an artillery officer whose skill on the front lines is matched by her total dedication to the cause. She is a no-nonsense revolutionary, a hardened soldier serving in a front-line unit of the Red Army.

Anna is also a Jewess. Tender, delicate, with "swarthily rosy cheeks" and "June azure in the whiteness of her eyes, and the bottomless depth of her black irises." She is a Jewess whose sex appeal is obvious even in a drab uniform and in the midst of the bloody, endless battle against Ukrainian counter-revolutionaries. She is an exciting woman whose serenity under fire belies a feminine appeal to male assertiveness and protection.

Bunchuk, the young officer in those command she is placed, falls in love with her almost at first sight. Their relationship grows during Bunchuk's illness as the Jewess nurses him back to health with all the skill, dedication, and maternal affection of typical Jewesses. The initial strangeness between the young Cossack and the lovely Jewess passes, and the two find themselves deeply in love. Bunchuk now blissfully discovers the passion and tenderness of a Jewess's love: "not only the caress and fire of a woman, but the warm, full-flowing care of a mother."[2]

Anna becomes pregnant and the two lovers daydream about the day when the war will end and Anna will be a happy mother and the proud wife of a national figure. She will be a busy housewife, cleaning and shopping, and there will be a happy future of peace and security for their child, a lovely, strong child with beautiful eyes like its mother.

The next day there is a surprise attack, and the Reds retreat in great confusion. All seems lost. Anna inspires a contingent of the artillery to follow her in confronting the enemy. She leads the men in a successful counter-attack until the tide of battle turns in the Reds' favor. Suddenly, Anna is hit by a shell and mortally wounded. By the time Bunchuk reaches her, she is covered by blood and in violent pain.

Ilya Bunchuk, the Cossack, is shattered by the Jewess's tragedy. Above and beyond personal pain at seeing the violent death of the woman he loved, there is the incomprehensibility of its senselessness. He cannot understand the relationship between her relevance to life and its brutal negation. Her relevance was vital and real, and central to Bunchuk's own reality. With the violent explosion of Anna's body into bloody fragments, the meaning of existence for Bunchuk has disintegrated.

Anna the Bolshevik was aware of the dilemma caused by her Jewishness. Her reluctance to answer Bunchuk's questions about her nationality, her disappointment when he guessed she was Jewish, and her unease about the revealing signs indicate a familiar sensitivity on the subject of Jewishness. Obviously from her response and from Bunchuk's hint of the Jews' "reputation," anti-Semitic prejudice was operative even at this early, idealistic stage of the Bolshevik Revolution. The charge that "the Jews do all the ordering and don't go under fire themselves" was a standard cry, and Jews felt called upon to prove time and again that it was not true.

J.-P. Sartre writes about this aspect of anti-Semitism and the Jew:

> Even if he has passed the military age, he is going to feel the necessity of enlisting—whether he does anything about it or not—because people are pretending everywhere that Jews are slackers. . . . Now this referred to the beginning of the war of 1914, and Austria had had no war since that of 1866, which was carried on with a professional army. This slander upon the Austrian Jews, which has been spread in France also, is simply the spontaneous fruit of distrust of the Jew.
>
> In 1938, at the time of the international crisis that was resolved at Munich, the French government called up only certain categories of the reserve. The majority of the men able to bear arms were not yet mobilized. Already, however, stones were being thrown through the store windows of one of my friends, a Jewish merchant at Belleville, on the grounds that he was a slacker. Thus the Jew, if he is to be left in peace, should be mobilized ahead of other people. . . .[3]

In literature it was up to the Jewess to prove the charge untrue. It was her natural prerogative to counter the negative image of the Jew whatever that image happened to be. In the first decades of the twentieth century, one charge, among others, was that the Jew shirked his civic duties. Here Anna fills the role of counter-stereotype; she is the Bolshevik heroine, the nonshirker Jew.

The shirker-Jew myth is a twentieth-century phenomenon. It is a by-product of his citizenship. In earlier ages when the Jew had neither liberty nor rights, no civic duties were expected of him. It took several decades of Jewish integration into Gentile society for the Gentile to create this myth.

This new myth went hand in hand with the use of the Jew as scapegoat. The Jew as shirker caused Germany's colossal defeat in World War I. So went a popular cry in the Weimar Republic, which served as one of the elements of early Hitlerian propaganda.

And the Jew, traumatized by onuses throughout his history among the Gentiles, attempts to defend himself although he is not quite certain of the nature of the charge. He believes he has been a model citizen: he knows he tries harder. The charge of shirking is just as confusing as it is painful. How should he defend himself?

> Since the Jew is dependent upon opinion for his profession, his rights, and his life, his situation is completely unstable. Legally not open to attack, he is at the mercy of the whims and passions of the "real" society. He carefully watches the progress of anti-Semitism; he tries to foresee crises and gauge trends in the same way that the peasant keeps watch on the weather and predicts storms. He ceaselessly calculates the effects that external events will have on his own

> position. He may accumulate legal guarantees, riches, honors; he is only the more vulnerable on that account, and he knows it. Thus it seems to him at one and the same time that his efforts are always crowned with success—for he knows the astonishing successes of his race—and that a curse has made them empty, for he will never acquire the security enjoyed by the most humble Christian.[4]

Like the hero in Franz Kafka's novel *The Trial* (1925), the Jew feels he is on perpetual trial; he does not know the charge, nor does he know his judges or the date of the trial because it is continually delayed. To prepare his defense he keeps adopting different positions, reevaluating and improving old ones. But the insecurity of his position, the nonexplicitness of the charge, erodes his self-assurance and, finally, without a trial ever having taken place, he is led off and killed.

Nor does Anna Pogoodko's heroism save her from ultimate destruction. On the contrary, the very fact of her Jewishness predisposes Anna to a tragic fate. Her role as a Communist comrade, a Red heroine, does not alter this destiny. Her death is inevitable.

The violence of her death, its savage brutality is, however, new. Violence administered to the beautiful, heroic woman carrying in her body the seed of a new life—this is a frightening new element, a frightening premonition. A re-enactment of past massacres and pogroms, this bloody scene in a modern framework seems like a microcosm of the vast catastrophe to befall European Jewry within two decades.

Sholokhov was not alone in his choice of violence as a culmination to the Jewess's role. Chirikov's play *The Jews,* discussed earlier, presents the Jewess Leah in a similar context. Her death was likewise one of those ghastly spectacles that while shocking the viewer predispose him to the acceptance of even more horror.

Chirikov's death scene was inspired by the 1903 pogrom in Kishinev. That bloody massacre at the dawn of a new century was not only a continuation of those that preceded it but a foretaste of others to come in twentieth-century Russia, making the grisly years of the Communist Revolution a welcome relief for Russian Jewry. The years of the counter-revolution, between 1919 and 1921, were once more a series of nightmares for Jews. The name of Ukrainian national hero Simon Petlura is written on the pages of Jewish history in the blood of women and children. In 1919 alone, 493 pogroms were perpetrated by his men, killing over 70,000 Jews in the Ukraine. At the end of that summer General Denikin's White Army continued the massacre. By the end of the hostilities in 1921 a quarter of a million Jews had perished in Kiev and the surrounding area.

Had not this incident prepared the ground for the massacre of Babi Yar, outside Kiev, only twenty years later? Post-Holocaust audiences watch with horror documentary films showing compliant rows of Jews meekly marching into the firing line of Nazi guns at the ravine's edge. How is this possible? Why? Why on earth do they march unresisting? Perhaps the answer lies in the massacres that preceeded it, and the scars they left on Jewish mentality.

The scars of victimization, the sense of helplessness and futility, stemmed in Russia in large measure from the 1880s when Czar Alexander III launched a project of officially instituted pogroms for the elimination of the "Jewish problem." In Hitler's program, the "Final Solution," only the term was new. From the 1880s the systematic massacre of defenseless civilians passively observed, patiently tolerated, by the rest of the world became an institution, an integral part of the Russian scene—and a major element in the prelude to the Holocaust.

Jewish toleration of violence was equally dangerous. It had perhaps as significant a role as the violence-toleration of the rest of the world in inspiring Hitler, the initiator of the great massacre. The Jews' "familiarity" with suffering inflicted by Christians, their fatalistic acceptance of pain, and their "it, too, shall pass" optimism in the face of ghastly atrocities, greatly contributed to the totality of the Jewish catastrophe. How many Jews could have saved themselves during the Holocaust had they not "expected" a certain amount of physical abuse from Christians?

British novelist Joseph Hatton's *By Order of the Czar* (1890) deals with the implications of the cruel 1880s in the life of Russian Jewry through the medium of lovely and regal Anna Klosstock, nicknamed "Queen of the Ghetto." During a pogrom in her native town, Anna witnesses the torture of her father, the murder of her fiancé, and the massacre of her friends and relatives. She herself is raped, then publicly knouted by the governor of the district, General Petronovich. The unfortunate Jewess survives all this but is transformed into an embittered savage obsessed with the thought of revenge. She is unrecognizable: all who had known her and admired her beauty now turn with horror from the brutalized Jewess who is incapable of any emotion except a nihilistic rage. In her quest for revenge, Anna Klosstock joins the Socialists and plunges, body and soul, into their clandestine preparations to overthrow the regime of the czar.

Hatton seems to be saying: Look what have you done to the Jew! Your abuses have turned him into an inhuman savage. If he is a Socialist, if he is a nihilist, if he is plotting to overthrow regimes, it is not entirely his fault: his propensity for trouble-making is justifiable.

The best-intentioned Christian readers of the best-intentioned Christian writers like Hatton would be inclined to accept this thesis and not stop to ask: is the Jew indeed a Socialist, a nihilist, a plotter, a troublemaker, more than any Christian? Does he indeed do mischief because he is driven to doing mischief? Does he indeed react actively to Christian abuse?

Has the Jew ever reacted to abuse in a way that could be considered an authentic human response? Throughout history, throughout his sojourn among the Gentiles, the Jew believed in silent, passive suffering as a means of survival. He adopted passivity as a moral value. The Christian preached "turning the other cheek"; the Jew practiced it. The Jew chose to absorb physical and mental assault without retaliating.

The savage assault of the Crusader was greeted by meek submission. Entire Jewish communities along the Seine, the Rhine, and the Danube awaited their murderers with prayer. The pyres of the Inquisition snuffed out Jewish lives that were, like burnt sacrifices, offered humbly, without protest. Pillage, rape, and massacre by generations of pogromists were borne in silence by Jews who believed suffering expiates sin. Jews throughout their history in the Diaspora believed that the silent agony of mangled children, disemboweled women, and tortured men glorified the name of God. Kiddush Hashem, the Sanctification of the Name, became the ultimate virtue. The Jewish death cry—Shema Ysrael . . . Hear O Israel . . . God is One!—was the only outcry, the only physical response to inhuman violence meted out by Christians.

The baffling nonresponse of the Jew confused, and troubled, the Christian. The Jew's historic passivity in the face of Christian abuse could only create confusion and guilt in the mind of the Christian. Even those Christians who did not directly participate in the administration of the abuse were aware of the suffering inflicted on Jews, and rightfully expected a predictable response. And when the Jew, inexplicably, remained passive, the Christian had no choice but to invent a response he considered authentic. In the absence of visible retaliation, the Christian assumed the Jew struck back invisibly: secretly he poisoned wells to bring the plague upon the Christian populace; under cover of darkness he murdered Christian children in order to extract their blood for the Passover matzo; at night he sneaked into the church to pierce the host in order to desecrate it; and he conspired to take over the Christian world in order to punish it by enslavement and exploitation. Christian guilt has been a major factor in the process of anti-Jewish myth-making.

The myth of Jewish conspiracy to take over the world had wide credence in turn-of-the century Europe, and even America. French, German, English, and American fiction disclosed the sinister secret: international Jewry was plotting to subjugate Christianity, international Jewish banking was plotting to bankrupt the world economy, and international Zionism was plotting to overthrow all legitimate regimes.

The Jewish world conspiracy myth appeared on the shores of the New World in 1891 in Ignatius Donelly's novel *Caesar's Column, a Story of the Twentieth Century,* in which the Jews are invincible characters of greed and an unscrupulous drive for power.

Donelly's book predated the publication of the infamous *Protocols of the Elders of Zion* under the auspices of the last czar. This pamphlet, a series of "minutes" by alleged Zionist leaders who met at night in Jewish cemeteries to plan the take-over of the Christian world by wiles and lies, survived with astonishing vigor up to our day, despite official proof that it was a fraud. In 1921 when the *Times* of London disclosed it as a forgery, *The Protocols* made a dramatic debut in the United States. Auto magnate Henry Ford publicized it in the *Dearborn Independent,* liberally citing passages and, editorializing on its contents, warned of the "Jewish menace." Reprints of the pamphlet appeared in Boston under the title *Protocols and World Revolution,* and in New York, *Praemonitus Praemunitus.*

The conspiracy myth gave a frightening dimension to a simultaneous myth of Judaism as an inferior race. The racist myth singled out the Jew as an object of contempt; the conspiracy myth singled him out as an object of fear. Ever since the appearance of Comte de Gobineau's *Essay on the Inequality of the Human Races* (1855), with its implications of the Jew's racial inferiority, the idea had caught on as a rationale for renewed Jew-hatred. It evolved into a popular myth decades before the emergence of Nazism.

Edouard Drumont utilized the three modern Jew-myths in *La France Juive* (1886), a pseudo-historical document which attempted to "prove" that the Jews were responsible for all of France's past and current ills and were planning to follow their destruction of Christianity by a mastery of the world. Drumont believed it to be his Christian duty to strike at the Jews: "I have prayed to Christ," he said, "for resignation if the publication of this book resulted for me in suffering, and for humility if my efforts were crowned with success. . . . God has taken the book under His care, because He knew, no doubt, that it was inspired by love of justice."[5]

Drumont's efforts were indeed crowned with success. His book became a blueprint of anti-Semitism in the pre-Nazi period, and later it was adopted as a guideline for the persecution and murder of Jews by a most prominent disciple—Adolf Hitler. In stating his purpose in his own catechism of hate, *Mein Kampf* (1924), Hitler expressed himself in almost identical terms: "I believe today that my conduct is in accordance with the will of the Almighty Creator. In standing guard against the Jews, I am defending the handiwork of the Lord."[6]

The Christian zeal displayed by Hitler's mentor in his anti-Jewish campaign was lauded by the French clergy. One wrote in an editorial in *Le Monde*: "All right-minded people will sympathize with the Sergeant of Jesus Christ, and will thank him for his intrepidity."[7] Another, a missionary priest, told the readers of *L'Univers*[8] that Drumont advocated "not the extermination of the Jews but the more or less violent expropriation of Jewish property." The "more or less violent expropriation" was visualized by Drumont as a pogrom:

> "On the day when the Catholics, weary of defending a society which has become exclusively Jewish[9] allow the hungry mob to march on the mansions of Jewish bankers . . . these beggars of yesterday, now the tyrants of today, will be crushed, and their blood will not make a stain any redder than the Kosher meat which they eat."[10]

La France Juive became a best seller. The foreign rights to the book were quickly snatched up. Catholic countries like Spain and Poland received them almost free: "This is the least I can do," wrote Drumont "for a country like Spain, which originated the tribunal of the Inquisition, a tribunal, patriotic and humane, which the Jews have attacked because it protected Christian honesty against the invading and exploiting Semite." Referring to Poland, he prayed: "Please God that my work may revive in the soul of every Polish patriot hatred for those infamous Jews who have betrayed them." Drumont's prayer was granted. Fifty years later many Poles proved it by volunteering for the Einsatzgruppen whose job it was to carry out under Gestapo orders the mass slaughter of Polish Jewry. In Austria the effect of Drumont's book was such that in 1886 a right-wing politician proposed that the Imperial Court should "offer premiums for shooting Jews similar to that offered for shooting wolves."[11] A newspaper editor wrote to Drumont:

> We Austrian anti-Semites, keeping up the unequal fight against the omnipotent Jew, had scarcely ventured to hope for this help coming from a country which we believed almost safe from the sinister influence of those people. France, with fifty to sixty thousand Jews, seemed to us an El Dorado in comparison with our country which

> is exploited by one and three quarter million individuals of that race.[12]

There is no doubt that the anti-Jewish outburst during the Dreyfus Affair, or perhaps the Affair itself, was a direct outcome of such anti-Semitic agitation. Pamphlets, circulars, editorials, letters to editors poured venom on Jews with unprecedented intensity. One letter-writer indicated that he wished to have "a rug made of the skin of a Jew."[13]

This in 1894, in France. Once again predating the Nazi program by half a century.

The manifesto of the French Catholic Party printed in the Catholic journal *La Croix* during the 1898 elections, which declared "We will vote only for candidates who will undertake to propose, support and vote for a law forbidding Jews to vote, or hold any military or civil office in the State," is reminiscent of Julius Streicher's defense at the Nüremberg trials, according to which he "had always only propagated the idea that the Jews, because of their alien character, should be removed from German national and economic life and withdrawn from close association with the body of the German people."[14]

Malcolm Hay, the Catholic historian, calls these precursors of Nazi ideology the "Godfathers of Belsen." Whether directly or indirectly, each contributed in his own way to an aberration of human values, a breakdown of civilization: the construction of gas chambers.

Ernest Renan, the French historian and Oriental scholar, was more explicit than Gobineau about the "incomplete race" of "the Semites" who, he claimed, "never had any comprehension of civilization." Renan went on to describe the "Semites" in the stereotypical terms of the Jew villain as selfish, intolerant, cowardly, and possessing an alien morality, whereas "to the Indo-European race belonged almost all the great military, political, and intellectual movements of the world."[15]

Composer Richard Wagner also believed that the Jew was incapable of creativity and, together with his son-in-law, Houston S. Chamberlain, waged a campaign to protect "Indo-European culture" from the "Semitic race." He warned German statesmen against Jewish domination:

> What a wonderful incomparable phenomenon is the Jew: Protean demon of humanity's decadence now triumphantly secure, and, in addition, a German citizen of Mosaic religion. . . . I most certainly regard the Jewish race as the born enemy of pure men and of all nobility in them, and am convinced that we Germans in particular will be destroyed by them.[16]

Chamberlain, in his extensive historical evaluation of world civilization, "proved" that all contributions to culture and humanity were made exclusively by Germanic races. The Bible was written by Aryans and published by Jews under false authorship. Even Jesus was an Aryan: the Jews simply expropriated him by forging the data of his origins.[17]

Wagner's "protean demon" appeared also in early twentieth-century German fiction. A "typical" Jewish family, August Hauschner's *Familie Losowitz* (1908), is a band of liars and cheats. Carl Hauptmann's *Israel Friedmann* (1913) is an unreliable character because his father was a Jew; and Arthur Dinter's Gentile protagonist commits a *Sin Against the Blood* (1918), a major Nazi taboo, by marrying a Jewish woman.

These writers continued in the tradition of nineteenth-century German romanticists who glorified the German peasant, rooted in the soil of the Vaterland, as opposed to the city resident who carried the stigma of despoiler. The idealization of the Volk automatically implied the vilification of the Jew, the urban dweller who had no roots in the German soil. The glorification of barbaric German prehistory implied denunciation of the modern era in which the Jew had an equal share of accomplishment. Many of these writers discarded the facade of romantic nationalism and attacked the Jew directly. Hitler describes with pathos the impact on his thinking of these novels, singling out Wilhelm von Polenz's *Büttnerbauer* (1906) as the book which drew his attention to the figure of the evil Jew. Through Polenz's vilified view Hitler related to Jews he saw on the streets of Vienna in his youth, and felt an instant hatred towards them.

The Jewess, however, did not become an evil figure in literature. On the contrary, Romantic fascination with Aryan values found a place of honor for the Jewess. While the Jew villain was invigorated anew in this age of frantic anti-Semitism, the Jewess remained untainted by the charge of racial evil, just as she had stood aloof of the taint of religious evil.

Volk romanticist Felix Dahn even presented an example of Aryan valor in the figure of a Jewess in *Ein Kampf Um Rom* (1904). The novel, a popular sample of period literature, waxed mawkish in its glorification of the Germanic pagan past and its contemporary representative, the German peasant.

The story takes place during the early centuries of the Christian era when the tall, proud, blond Goths rule Rome. The enchantingly beautiful Miriam, daughter of the Jew Isaac (who, by the way is a good Jew; such a good Jew that he is a rabid anti-Semite and despises all the other Jews in the novel—the puny, cowardly, "typical" traitorous Jews), is in love with handsome Totila, king of the Goths. The Jewess worships the great hero secretly from afar. She is, however, fortunate enough to get a chance to prove her love for the Goth.

Having by chance discovered that the Vandals plan a surprise attack, Miriam risks her life to warn Totila. Through her timely intervention, his honor and his people are saved. But Miriam, meanwhile, returning to her own people, is captured by the Vandals who guess her treachery and punish her by torture and execution.

Dahn's Miriam and Sholokov's Anna fulfil identical roles. Both are token Jews in un-Jewish roles: they prove the possibility of Jewish courage and love of fatherland. Both accomplish it as symbols should: beyond and above expectations.

Both are victimized women and victimized Jews. Their undeserved tragic fate cries out for protest, and because none is voiced, it, too, becomes an ingredient in the atmosphere of violence toleration. The senseless bloody brutality of their deaths seems somehow Jewish. These deaths are unrelated to the theme of Jewess-Christian confrontation, they seem, rather, central to the heroines' relevance as Jews. The message seems to be that Jews, even good, loyal, brave Jews, are properly subject to ruthless abuse. It need not be deserved. Jewishness alone qualifies one for a violent fate.

It had been the Jewish fate for centuries; it was one of the keystones of passivity in the face of every incident of anti-Jewish violence, until it culminated in the multiplication of violent episodes six million times.

Tragic figures of kind, brave, beautiful Jewesses of yesterday were still vivid in public memory. The names of beautiful Esterka from the fourteenth, "Golden Rose" from the seventeenth, and radiant Adel from the eighteenth century still haunted the public consciousness.

It was not only the harsh climate of eastern Europe that yielded names of persecuted and martyred Jewish women; the idyllic lands of the Arabian Nights are also stained by Jewish blood cruelly spilt—often the blood of young girls who resisted either sexual or religious abuse. Some, like the Jewess who consented to become the paramour of the Dey of Oran but refused to accept Islam, were publicly executed. The grave of another, the lovely seventeen-year-old Suleica Hatwil of Fez, Morocco, who similarly resisted conversion to Islam, became a popular shrine venerated today by Jews and Muslims alike—a unique phenomenon especially since Muslims as a rule do not venerate women. In the town of Arbel in Iraq, local people still tell the tale of a beautiful Jewess's gruesome execution for refusing to convert to Islam and become the wife of the town elder. Some chose to commit suicide rather than submit to humiliation and death. In the Persian city of Shiraz, a respectable member of the Muslim hierarchy imprisoned a beautiful Jewess in the mufti's palace until she would break down and consent to conversion and marriage. The young woman leaped from the window of the palace to the rocky depth of a gorge. In Constantinople, Yafta Abira was abducted from the home of her father, a well-to-do Jewish merchant, and confined in the royal palace where her betrothal to the sultan was celebrated. According to custom, the royal bridegroom presented the reluctant bride with a silk scarf, as token of their engagement. After the ceremony, in the privacy of her room, Yafta hanged herself with the scarf. In deference to her martyrdom, the sultan allowed her body to be buried in the Constantinople Jewish cemetery.

Incidents of Jewish martyrdom had served Christian literature for centuries: it is the raw material of which tragic Jewish heroines are made. Death had been a familiar affair with beautiful young Jewesses ever since their first appearance on the pages of fiction. It was romance-related: it proceeded directly from their confrontation with the Christian lover. The last decades of the nineteenth century however altered the pattern to include random violence unrelated to the theme of problematic Jewess-Christian romance. In these works violence committed against the Jewess seems to be an end in itself. In this emergent pattern, violence and death seem intrinsic not to the plot but to the Jewess figure: they are an integral part of her fabric. The tragedy of Chirikov's Leah, Hatton's Anna Klosstock, Sholokhov's Anna Pogoodko and Dahn's Miriam evokes the darkest periods of the Jewish historical experience—the crusades, ritual murder charges, pogroms—and, simultaneously, heralds the advent of an even darker era by reflecting the mood of growing violent Jew-hatred.

Even those Gentile writers who genuinely regretted this development continued to use the theme of violence. Thus, however unintentionally, they condoned violence against the Jew. Jewish suffering, history-proven, became a routine factor. A fatal companion to the growing anti-Semitic agitation on the part of conscious Jew-haters, this silent tolerance of unjust and undeserved Jewish suffering predisposed Jewish sympathizers to passivity in the face of the coming genocide. Christians who abhorred cruelty and violence, when faced with unspeakable Nazi abuses, continued their silence.

Tragically, toleration of violence became part of the Jews' mental world, as well. Ironically, they, too, came to believe that suffering was a Jewish condition. Acceptance of pain as inevitable paralyzed them in the face of the "Final Solution."

The greatest philo-Semites contributed to this atmosphere. The liberal Russian poet Maxim Gorki's "Massacre of Jews" (1904) is a graphic example. The ghastly spectacle of a pogrom's aftermath moves Gorki to see the Jew as the Eternal Sufferer forever wandering among the nations, exposed to their murderous whims, forever massacred, forever bled, wandering on towards a future of unending bloody abuse.

Paul Mühsam, a German liberal poet, in his indictment of war comments in a similar vein. In a post-World War I poem, "Der ewige Jude" (The Eternal Jew, 1924), the poet sees Ahasuerus, the eternally Wandering Jew, hovering above the deserted battlefield. The war has ended and corpses are scattered in tragic disarray, their silence a mute testimony of futility. The futility of human sacrifice spells hopelessness for the future of mankind. Man's pessimism is symbolized by the Wandering Jew: the human tragedy is precipitated in the destiny of the Jews. Ahasuerus sees it all: there is no solution possible for Jewish survival. Even Zionism, the movement which proposed an answer through the establishment of a Jewish state as haven from persecution, fails to promise hope. There is no hope of ever achieving that aim: the Jews are destined to be homeless. The Jewish fatherland is an impossible dream.

The Jew, in the post-Holocaust era, must consciously struggle against this paralyzing self-image of himself as predestined victim. He must unlearn centuries of indoctrination, presented through all forms of literary expression, which molded his self-image as eternal sufferer, as universal scapegoat for the ills of the world, as homeless wanderer. He has a fatherland. His wandering and persecution are at an end. Senseless suffering is no more the prerogative of the Jew than of any other nation. The Jew must learn to accept this and reach out for life without fear and without apology, without looking for approval and consent from the Gentile world. For there is no longer a "Gentile world"—just a world of the human family, a world of suffering and striving mankind.

Once this is accomplished, the Jewess will cease to be a symbol, whether as victim of ritual murder like Marlowe's Abigail, model of Enlightenment like Lessing's Recha, Romantic casualty like Scott's Rebecca, champion of assimilation like De Bonnières' Lia or of Zionism like Enacryos's Rachel, sex object par excellence like the "Belle Juive," or token patriot like Sholokhov's Anna. The Jewess will cease to be a defender of Judaism.

The twentieth century, although ushered in with unprecedented violence, will perhaps prove to be the century when the Jew will truly arrive, when the struggle for acceptance will end for him, the citizen of his own land, and when his right to that land, to his culture, to his religion—to life itself—will no longer be disputed by others. Then the Jewess of literature will be indistinguishable from other fictional heroines.

8

The Twentieth Century

> Where a woman is both beautiful and wise, there is one. Their blood is lively in whatever frame it flows, and when the frame is gone, its very dust enriches the still kindly soil. Their spirit is born anew in every generation. They are no more and yet they live forever.[1]

For a Jew the twentieth century is like a world rent in two by a violent volcanic eruption. The Holocaust, an explosion of accumulated turbulent trends, rocked twentieth-century civilization to its core and devastated European Jewry. The unprecedented fury of the eruption changed the face of the earth, and its impact continues to wreak havoc with established human values, political realities, and geographic configurations. The conflagration scorched humanity severely; Jewry was all but consumed in the flames.

A new Jewish nation rose from the ashes of death and destruction. This new people and this new state are but a sculpture of cinders, a body of burnt particles with a new soul: but a body perhaps toughened, perhaps wisened by the fire.

The twentieth century is two epochs. An abyss separates the pre-Holocaust era from the post-Holocaust period. Though the seeds of the Holocaust sprouted in the twentieth century, they were planted long ago by the earliest manifestations of anti-Semitism, by the first stirrings of hate. It is our duty now to redeem the past and assume responsibility for the future, to search for understanding of our historical experience. We must search for clues in issues and attitudes of recent memory. To understand the twentieth century, it is important to recall its beginnings.

What were the attitudes and issues at the turn of the century that resulted in the violent blowout of civilization? Was there an awareness of the approaching catastrophe? Were the volcanic rumblings recorded in literature?

As we have seen, increasing violence and its increasing tolerance were amply documented through the figures of Jewesses, each standing for a specific event in the progression of doom. Joseph Hatton's Anna Klosstock is the tortured spirit of czarist persecutions. Chirikov's Leah is the tragic victim of modern Jewry's agonized identity crisis, brutally solved by the pogrom of Kishinev. The Communist Revolution has its Jewish heroine in Anna Pogoodko, through whom Sholokhov gives eloquent evidence of the futility of Jewish efforts at integration even in the new Soviet era.

What was the picture like elsewhere, in other parts of the world with more liberal attitudes? Were we to focus a searchlight upon Germany for instance, the center stage of the twentieth-century Jewish drama, what would stand out in clear lines against the background? In the Germany of pre-Nazi decades the national feast of self-glorification, the Volk-centered culture, did not allow much room for the Jew. The literature of the age was characterized by the token Jew as German patriot, almost hysterical in his loyalty to the German fatherland, and by a growing number of Jew villains as emphatic counterpoints. Felix Dahn's Miriam, the Jewess infatuated with Totila, the Aryan demigod, who sacrifices her life for this embodiment of Germanism, and thus for Germanic values, is the symbol of that era. In the German mind she stands for the Jew as "liberal" Germans expected him to be and as "liberal" German Jews saw themselves.

But that was not the entire picture. Within the Jewish community the torment of identity continued despite the struggle of a century and a half for assimilation and acceptance. The history of German antagonism, first Christian, then Aryan, left on the Jew indelible marks of insecurity, self-hate, and despair, even if he happened to belong to the prosperous middle class. Of this phenomenon only Jewish writers were in a position to give an accurate account; Christians did not penetrate the inner Jewish world.

Georg Hermann's works, for instance, reveal the Jewish reality in the German fatherland before Hitler's onslaught terminated it. His novel *Jettchen Gebert* (1906) and its sequel, *Henriette Jacoby* (1908), were considered "the Jewish Buddenbrooks," with their period sketches and portrayal of Berlin's cultured Jewish society.

Jettchen is the counterpart of Chirikov's Leah. Her ghetto is a glittering Berlin Jewish milieu; her illusory avenue of escape is also a young Gentile student. Jettchen's ambivalence toward Judaism and its tragic outcome parallel that of Leah: both Jewish heroines are symbols of pre-Holocaust Jewry and their roles foreshadow the great Jewish catastrophe.

The novel *Jettchen Gebert* centers on the figure of the lovely, bright Jettchen who, although engaged to be married to a Jewish merchant, falls in love with a young German poet. Her father, the indulgent Jewish papa of the age, a well-to-do petit bourgeois, is happy and proud with the way things are turning out for his beloved daughter. A big wedding is planned, an elaborate trousseau is prepared. He is convinced of Jettchen's happiness. After all, he has done everything for her that his noveau riche capacity can provide. He has arranged a stable future for her with an eligible, kind-hearted, wealthy young businessman.

Little does he know that Jettchen's well-ordered security is threatened by a Christian, a bedraggled, starving poet-scholar named össling.. Little does he realize that Jettchen is secretly yearning to turn her back on the material security of the old-fashioned Jewish home. The well-mannered, beautiful, cultured Jettchen, the apple of Mr. Gebert's eye, cheerfully prepares for the lavish wedding, excitedly tries on the elegant wedding gown. When the opulent wedding ceremony is about to begin, the beautiful bride commits suicide.

It is no longer the promise of a better life beyond the walls of the ghetto which urges the Jewess to flee. Materially, the Jew had "arrived" during the latter half of the nineteenth century. Yet the Jew's sense of alienation is devastating, and the lure of the Gentile world is just as powerful as ever. The bedraggled young Gentile represents the impossible dream. The goal is still, even in the first decade of the twentieth century, beyond reach. The dream is still impossible for the Jewess as long as she remains a Jew. In the decades before the rise of Hitler, the Jew remained alienated in Gentile society. It was as if emancipation had been an ambiguous gift. To be sure, there was social integration in housing, in education, in jobs. There were social clubs which accepted Jews. There were political offices open to Jews. And there was wide-scale intermarriage. But there were many more schools, jobs, social and professional associations, neighborhoods, which rejected the Jew. The atmosphere was antagonistic. Anti-Jewish prejudices were deeply rooted, while tolerance was a token, skin-deep, sporadic phenomenon. And the Jew sensed a growing hostility.

His hunches were right. The rise of Hitler wiped away in one sweep the carefully nurtured, paper-thin layer of tolerance. And this time there was no escape for the Jew. Not even the ultimate surrender of Jewish identity, conversion to Christianity, provided a solution. A Jew was condemned not for rejecting Christianity but for being a Jew. Judaism became an inherent, inescapable source of destruction.

The conflict between Judaism and Christianity ended with the appearance of Hitlerian Nazism. The age-old dilemma had ceased, in a sense: it was no longer a question of choice. The Jew's rejection was total, his status non-negotiable. No more was he told as in the Middle Ages, "convert and you can live," "become a Christian and you can become a fellowman"; or as during the period of Enlightenment, "assimilate and you will be liberated, cease being a Jew and you will become a human being"; or as during the rise of European nationalism, "become a Frenchman, an Englishman, a German, an Austrian, a Hungarian . . . and you can stay among us," "give up your Jewish loyalties, your traditions, your identity, and we will consider you a true patriot." For as long as the Jew remained a Jew, he was not a fellowman in the Christian sense, a true human being in the "enlightened" sense, nor a true patriot in the nationalistic sense. He was a Jew. He remained "beyond the pale." But now there were no preconditions for acceptance. Now the Jew was told: "you are a Jew, you are unacceptable; you are a Jew, you cannot live."

Now survival became the impossible dream. The escape was no longer from the chains and restrictions of Jewish tradition, or from the walls of the ghetto: now the Jew had to flee for his life.

But where could the Jew flee?

German author Alfred Andersch grapples with this Jewish dilemma through the figure of the Jewess, Judith, in his novel, *Sansibar, oder der letzte Grund* (1965). Judith is the Jewess myth of the Holocaust. She has dark, long, flowing hair, enormous, black, brilliant eyes, Semitic features, and a striking beauty. The place is Germany and the time is the Nazi era. Jewishness is synonymous with death. There are no redeemable aspects: the Jewess's womanhood has no value. Judith is fleeing from the Nazis through those channels of escape which still seem open. Special documents enable her to leave her town. Beyond the town danger lurks at every turn. Her flight is agonizing and endless, a continual string of nightmares. She is trying to get to Zanzibar, off the coast of East Africa, where she hopes to find haven.

But Zanzibar might as well be a distant planet, remote from the world of hostile humanity which persecutes and pursues her, which reviles and threatens and abuses her. Judith flees on. In fact, her flight ceases to be a flight in the physical sense: it is a state of mind, a nightmarish flight from fear. It is static and infinite; a condition rather than a motion.

The beautiful Jewess, her long dark hair flowing, flees on. Her courage, faith and perseverance ebb and flow: hope is a comforting or mocking companion, by turns friend and traitor. The world, the Gentile world, looks on, a passive blur or heavy stumbling block. More often, the dark pursuer. Safety and freedom are one step ahead of the Jewess. They are beyond the horizon.

The flight never ends. Persecution remains doggedly at Judith's heels; happiness and security beyond reach. The unattainability of both is implicit in the Jewess's flight. It is her fate, the Jew's classic tragedy.

In the New World, far from the nightmare of the German Reich, the Jew stood on the crossroads, as well. Ever since his arrival in the United States, the Jew did not cease the struggle for the security of acceptance. In literature his classic image, the imported negative stereotype, persisted. He had not yet achieved integration socially and economically when the storm clouds of Nazism began to rise on the European horizon. Apart from his concern for fellow Jews on the other side of the Atlantic, the American Jew had reason to be apprehensive about his own safety.

The threat of Nazism was real in America in the 1930s. Father Coughlin's broadcasts appealed to a wide segment of the populace, and the equation between "Godless" Communism and Jews, and between Fascism and patriotic American struggle against Communism was easy to make. Anti-Semitism, on the increase ever since the early years of the Depression, now took an overt upswing. Charles E. Coughlin's Christian Front movement recruited the majority of Irish-Americans. Many read without questioning his blatantly anti-Semitic editorials in the organization's journal, *Social Justice.* The Jews' mounting alarm for their fellow Jews in Europe was made through such rhetoric to seem like an unpatriotic tendency. Jewish agitation against Nazism drew vehement charges of interventionism. The popular American hero Charles Lindburgh warned that the Jews, prompted by self-interest, wanted to draw America into a disastrous war, and he was believed by many. Convinced of the accuracy of the charge, Ambassador Joseph P. Kennedy cautioned the film industry, which he believed was controlled by Jews, to desist from making anti-Nazi films. Senator Gerald Nye openly accused Hollywood of goading the nation into war with Germany.

Writers like Theodore Dreiser and George Sylvester Viereck had prepared the ground for virulent anti-Semitic propaganda through the import of European Jew villains. Dreiser's play *The Hand of the Potter* (1919) had included a Shylock-type owner of a boarding house whose callous greed for gold was deplored even by his own daughter, the stereotyped Jewish beauty. There was also an implication of ritual murder in the play. The central character, a demented twenty-one-year-old Jew, sexually abuses, then murders, an eleven-year-old Irish girl as she is returning from confession. During the 1930s and 1940s when anti-Nazi public opinion in America could have made the difference between life and death for the Jews of Europe, Dreiser and his associates campaigned against them. Precisely when every other gate was locked to Jews fleeing Nazi persecution, Dreiser and his friends caused the gates of "the land of liberty" to be shut as well. Through his influence as an editor of the *American Spectator,* he supported the anti-Jewish campaign; then, in 1944 when the majority of European Jews had been massacred, Dreiser expressed his sympathy.[2]

Dreiser's belated tribute was paralleled by Thomas Wolfe, who had not however lived to witness the Holocaust. He, too, found praise for dead Jews in his last novel, *You Can't Go Home Again,* published posthumously in 1940. His earlier novels contained less flattering portrayals of American Jews.

In *The Web and the Rock* (1938) we meet Esther, the prototype par excellence of the American Jewish "enabler." The novel centers in a Christian-Jewess relationship, set against the backdrop of affluent Jewish life in New York city. Esther is the beautiful and cultured wife of a New York businessman. The Christian is young Monk, a poor but talented country boy drifting aimlessly in the big city. When he meets the friendly, vivacious, intelligent Jewess, he is intoxicated by her charm. Elegant Esther, notwithstanding her sophistication, harbors the heart of a Jewish mother; the young Gentile's vulnerability appeals to her. She falls deeply in love with the guileless innocent; she discovers his literary talent and gives him the initiative to write. When her inspiration begins to bear fruit, Esther paves his way to literary success by arranging important contacts for him, and by introducing him to New York society.

Esther's relationship with the young Christian establishes his career but jeopardizes her personal life. While he climbs to fame and fortune, Esther compromises her reputation and the respectability of her home. Monk becomes an international celebrity and decides to enjoy his wide acclaim abroad. He embarks on a lecture tour of Europe where he is fawned upon by flocks of women. In the intoxicating atmosphere of social recognition he forgets the Jewess who was responsible for it all.

Esther withers away. She loses interest in her family, her social circle, her appearance, and begins to disintegrate. Unlike Chekhov's Anna, the nineteenth-century heroine who destroyed herself with tuberculosis, the twentieth-century American Jewess chooses a contemporary weapon. She drowns her grief and her life in alcohol. At the novel's end, while the Christian ex-lover is luxuriating in European pleasure spots, Esther, lost in a drunken stupor, sits on a Central Park bench. Dishevelled and shabby, the once radiant socialite "so full of life and health," mutters incoherently as the night patrol hauls her into jail for drunkenness and illegal loitering.

Thomas Wolfe's personal experience largely paralleled that of young Monk. He, too, found life among the intelligentsia and the rich of New York Jewry a dazzling experience after his small-town upbringing: he, too, was nurtured as a man and writer by the love of a brilliant, rich, exciting Jewess who helped his literary career by introducing him to wealthy and cultured Jews and their friends. As an instructor at the Washington Square campus of New York University, he came into intimate contact with Jewish youth. Their world, their aspirations, hopes, and fears were made real to him. Yet he, like his literary predecessors, continued to see the Jews not as people but symbols: the men, of evil, and the women, of sexual seduction:

> Again and again, a mad, distorted picture blazed within his mind. He saw a dark regiment of Jewish women in their lavish beauty, their faces melting into honey, their eyes glowing, their breasts like melons. . . . They were the living rack on which the trembling backs of all Christian lovers had been broken.[3]

Nor does this modern American author refer to the reality of the American Jewish condition. *The Web and the Rock* was published at the eve of World War II, five years after the rise of Hitler, three years after the promulgation of the Nüremberg Laws which disenfranchized German Jewry and started their wholesale exodus. Large numbers came to New York, and the tales they told traumatized American Jewry. The dread of doom hung in the air. Jewish writers echoed the rumblings of the volcano, but Thomas Wolfe's ear was tuned only to the sounds of the stereotyped rhythm: he echoed only these in his Jewish portrayals.

Wolfe's Esther is in fact the usual Romantic casualty: the Jewess who is destroyed by her love which nurtures the Christian. Her symbolic death is the unjust, undeserved fate of the Jew. Despite their ambition, culture, and wealth, American Jews were still victims of Gentile society.

American Jews reacted to the Nazi menace and its reverberations in their country the way their correligionists had to the rise of racist anti-Semitism in Europe half a century earlier. For some it was the clarion call for Jewish renaissance, a return to Jewish values —religious, cultural, or nationalist. Writers like Ludwig Lewisohn, Maurice Samuel, and Ben Hecht reawakened to their Jewish identity and portrayed the Jewish reality from this vantage point. They recognized the roots of their alienation and preached affirmation of Jewishness as a path to self-respect, and Zionism as a road to survival.

Others, having internalized Christian Jew-hatred, searched for identity with their negative self-image as starting point. The pathetic spectacle of Jewish self-hate was one of the most poignant phenomena of the American Jewish scene during an era when its reverse was Jewry's most urgent need. Writers like Michael Gold, Albert Halper, Budd Schulberg, and others saw the Jew as the Christian saw him, and described him with an authority Christian authors could not claim. And so, while most Christian authors continued to ignore Jewish reality and to use imported stereotypes, Jewish writers became either zealots of the Jewish cause or hysterical denouncers of everything Jewish, both incapable of coping objectively with Jewish reality.

But when from the cinders of the Holocaust a new Jewish state and people were born, American Jews had no difficulty in coming to grips with this new reality. You did not have to be a Zionist to identify with Israel. The brave Israeli soldier redeemed the image of the cowardly ghetto Jew. And the American Jew, the liberal, the patriot, the Socialist, felt the burden of that image lift from his assimilated shoulders. He could stop hating himself. He could stop denying his Jewishness. Now Jewish was beautiful.

Did the Christian share this view?

One of the most popular modern American writers, James Michener, erected a virtual monument to this new perspective of Jews and their history of his novel *The Source* (1965).

Michener's Jewish heroine, Vered Bar-El, is the embodiment of the best in the Jewess stereotype. Although a modern liberated woman and a scholar, she is the model of all the qualities that make up the woman ideal in Christian literature. Like Israel, the ancient-modern land, she is a dual image—biblical-modern: "she seemed to be the spirit of Israel, a dark-haired, lovely Jewess from Bible times."[4]

Dr. Vered Bar-El, the Israeli archeologist, meets Dr. John Cullinane, an American archeologist, at a dig he has come to conduct in Israel. Upon meeting her, Cullinane is immediately conscious of his colleague—"a small woman, beautiful, bright-eyed, a pleasure to have at any dig"[5]—as a sex object, Jewess style. And when the dig yields a small statue of Astarte, the Canaanite goddess of love, Cullinane is struck by the similiarity between the modern Jewess and the ancient goddess, a similarity not incidental. Dr. Bar-El herself is unaware of the mystical link between the ancient sex symbol and herself. When it is brought to her attention, she is baffled by the comparison:

> It was Astarte, the Canaanite goddess, and she reminded Cullinane of a little statue of Vered Bar-El. The naked little goddess with circular breasts was brought to Vered's table, and she said quietly, "I am sure I don't know how he could tell." So the boy tore his handkerchief and made an improvised bikini and halter for the clay goddess, and the antique little girl did look amazingly like the archaeologist, and probably for the same reason: that each represented the ultimate female quality, the sexual desire, the urge toward creation that can sometimes become so tangible in a bikini or in the work of a long-forgotten artist in clay.[6]

Romance buds slowly, tentatively between the Jewess and the Christian. Like Rebecca and Ivanhoe, each is keenly aware of his own role: each is at the core of a world molded by history. Indeed each *is* a separate world.

Contemporary Michener, just like nineteenth-century Scott, does not dispose of the Jewess-Christian dilemma by the Jewess's death. In coming to terms with their destiny, each withdraws into the confinement of his earlier world, and the wide gap between them becomes shockingly manifest. The Christian is wiser and sadder through his encounter with the phenomenon of the Jewess, and the Jewess is deeply affected by having loved and lost. The two go their separate ways:

> He kissed her passionately, as if he knew that this was the last time he would ever stand with her in the Galilean night, and for one brief moment she did not resist but remained close to him, like a little Astarte whose responsibility it was to remind men of love. Then, as if she were pushing away a part of her life which had become too precious to be carried carelessly, she forced her hands against his chest and slowly the Catholic and the Jew parted, like comets which had been drawn to each other momentarily but which must now seek their separate orbits.[7]

Cullinane returns to the United States, and Vered, sobered by the shattering implications of the romance with the Christian, goes off to marry a Jewish businessman, a man much older and lacking her intellectual sensitivity. But, she explains to the offended Christian, a

Jewess can "marry only a Jew."[8] There is the compelling historical bond—the suffering of Jews from the Babylonian exile in the sixth century B.C., to the Israeli Wars of Independence. To be a Jewess is to share Jewish past and future. To be a Jewess is to marry another Jew.

The compelling historical bond, Holocaust-induced, has a renewed urgency. Michener has perceived this relevance in the post-Holocaust psyche of the Jew. More than a solemn legacy, the Holocaust is a collective liability. It compels commitment to Jewish survival. It compels every Jew into a sworn brotherhood bound by its cataclysmic implications. The Jew, whether he wishes it or not, in relation to Jewish survival ceases to be an individual: his priorities as an individual must take second place if they are not identical with those that ensure the survival of his people. This awesome duty is the burden of the Holocaust.

How does this affect the age-old Jewess-Christian dilemma? James Michener's Jewess-Christian relationship remains true to stereotyped pattern: Christian and Jewess meet, love, and part. The rationale, however, has changed. No more does the love relationship end in the Jewess's ritual murder by an avenging Jew-father, nor in her rejection, or self-inflicted death, or terminal virginity because of the irreconcilable difference of religion. The Jewess does not sacrifice her love for the Christian on the altar of spiritual ideals. Post-Holocaust Jewish reality is stated in the harsh terms of Jewish survival.

American author Claude Brown was unaware of this modern Jewish reality in his treatment of the Jewish subject. In *Manchild in the Promised Land* (1965), Brown introduces the Jewess Judy Strump in what could be described as a stereotyped Jewess-Christian encounter. But Brown, an American black, sees it neither as Christian vis-à-vis Jewess, nor as the Jew vis-à-vis the Gentile world; he views it within the context of black-white relations in America. Claude, the black protagonist, meets Judy, the white liberal, and the two young people fall in love. Their six-month love affair, set against the background of New York City's ethnic realities, deepens into a friendship. But Judy's parents, alarmed at the prospect of losing their daughter to the world of the "goyim," succeed in breaking up the romance by sending Judy to stay at the home of relatives in Connecticut. Claude is not concerned with the Jewish problem. For him, the wound is white-inflicted.

It is also interesting, and quite revealing, to see the world of Jewish-Christian relations at the time through the eyes of a Jewish author. In his novel *The Assistant* (1957), Bernard Malamud likewise approaches the issue through the medium of a Jewess-Christian romance. The scene is a Brooklyn neighborhood inhabited by Italian-Americans and Jews. An uneasy truce exists between the two ethnic groups. Neither minority ever crosses the invisible dividing line that separates it from the other. Each lives locked in its own world of values and goals; communication is limited to the exchange of goods and services.

The Jew, Morris Bober, is a quiet, reserved man who spends endless working hours in his tiny and bare grocery store which provides a meager living for his family. It is this grocery store which becomes the stage for the drama of confrontation. The Christian is Frank Marusco, a no-good Italian drifter; the Jewess is Helen, the grocer's daughter. The two meet when Frank, for reasons of his own, becomes Bober's assistant.

Helen Bober, the Jewess, has a startling effect on Frank Marusco, the Christian. Although not typically "Jewish looking," Helen possesses those qualities of "sexiness" which are proverbially Jewish. Even her imperfections, her strange, wobbly walk, her slightly bowed legs, project Jewish eroticism. Frank is obsessed with her "special quality of sexiness." The Jewess's unattainability stirs a disquieting awareness of the distance between them, and his obsession deepens. His need for her nearness inspires him to emulate the serious, intelligent, and ambitious young woman, and he, too, becomes a more industrious worker, careful of his appearance and habits.

In time, Frank Marusco earns Helen's cautious friendship, and one evening the Jewish girl agrees to a date at the movies. Moments before Frank's arrival at their rendezvous in a Brooklyn park, Helen is brutally attacked by Frank's former crony, who has secretly lusted after his friend's Jewish girl. Frank gets to the scene in time to save Helen from rape. But when the traumatized Jewess, her blouse ripped above her breast, clings to him for comfort, Frank is unable to control himself. Seeing her partially exposed body and intoxicated by her nearness, his own long-repressed need bursts the carefully erected facade of propriety, and he rapes her. It is a desperate and tragic move. In violating her body, he violates her Jewishness. With a shock, Helen's sense of Jewishness awakens. The ethnic, religious, and social gap between them is now a gaping abyss. The beginnings of a bridge have been destroyed.

In the eyes of Helen Bober the act of rape in the Brooklyn park was a violence perpetrated against Jewesses of all ages in all the ghettos of the world—it was the rape of Judaism by Christianity.

The Jewess and Christian recede behind the confines of their respective worlds. She will never be the same. Having come into contact with Christianity, she ceases to be an individual: she becomes a symbol. Helen Bober, at the moment of her victimization, automatically assumes the Jewess role. So Jews throughout their history have reawakened to their Jewish identity at times of persecution.

But all is not lost in the Jewess-Christian encounter. The conventional pattern created by Christians of an earlier era undergoes modifications at Malamud's hands. The young Italian-American discovers that the real source of his infatuation was what Helen stood for—Jewish values and way of life. At the conclusion of the novel, Frank Marusco is preparing to undergo conversion to Judaism in order to share the Jewish world of Helen Bober.

The sharp rise in intermarriage during the post-Holocaust decades tells a great deal about the contemporary Jewish world and about Christian attitudes towards it. One of the factors is, of course, the loosening of religious ties on each side; another is the success of minorities in becoming Americanized, which undoubtedly eases the way across social boundary lines.

More important however is the change in Jewish self-image, and in the Christian response to that change. The Holocaust and the subsequent rise of the Jewish state created a new Jewishness. A new basis for identification was formed out of the trauma of collective death and rebirth. Perhaps it could be called pride. A nucleus of national pride was born, and it translated itself into an individual sense of belonging.

Jewish youth responded in various ways to this newborn national self-image. An emotional need to share in the adventure of nation-building prompted some to become pioneers in the new Jewish state. Others, curious about Jewish historical "roots," embarked on studies of Jewish subjects. Still others underwent a crisis of identity.

A new Jewish militancy was born. Young Jews banded into vigilante groups to defend "Jewish lives, Jewish honor." The battle of centuries was fought on local streets to undo the age-long myths of the Jew as a physical coward and a weakling. Age-long Jewish attitudes of pacifism were remolded into activism for Jewish causes. The demonstration of solidarity with every oppressed and persecuted Jewish group became a creed.

Some Gentiles responded to this development with alarm and resentment. In Madrid, Spain, where a small, rather recent, Jewish community leads an unobtrusive existence, Lazaro Montenero de la Puente embodied these negative reactions in a modern Raquel figure in his novel *Doña Fermosa* (1955). In this unusual adaptation of the Raquel-Alfonso theme, beautiful Raquel is a symbol of militant Jewish youth. Like her predecessors, this Raquel becomes Alfonso's mistress in order to save the Jews of Toledo. But unlike her predecessors, this Raquel is not beloved by the Spanish nation. On the contrary, her stubborn intransigence generates hostility among both Christians and Jews. Raquel's conduct causes both camps to conspire against her; her own father stands at the head of her indignant opponents, and finally it is he who takes the dramatic, fatal step to save Spain from her ruthless domination, and the Jews from disgrace: he knifes Raquel to death.

In a shocking role-switch, the twentieth-century Barabas, the daughter-killer Jew, is actually the hero. By turning the father into the agent of Christians, Puente transferred the role of villain from Jew to Jewess—probably the only such incident in literature of casting against type. The role-switch is, however, not complete. It is the Jewess, once again, who is subject to fatality. Sinner or saint, she is destined for doom.

Puente's reaction was not representative of Gentile response elsewhere. On the contrary, the overwhelming Gentile concensus was a new appreciation. Born partly out of Holocaust-induced guilt which compelled re-evaluation of attitudes, and partly out of genuine respect for the Jew's new self-image, the Christian began to approach the Jew from a position more akin to equality than ever before. A solution to the Christian-Jew dilemma now even included the possibility of the Christian's conversion to Judaism.

The State of Israel was a major motivating factor in such a trend. Numerous Christians have opted for life within the framework of Judaism after visiting Israel, the way Malamud's Frank Marusco does after his exposure to a Jewess. For others, the enormity of the Jewish catastrophe served as starting point on the road towards Judaism.

Jane MacDwyer, a young Irish-American Catholic, when confronted with evidence of Nazi atrocities, began her search for answers to the Jewish historical tragedy and this led her to the Jewish faith and land. In her autobiography, written years later in her Jerusalem home, MacDwyer, now Devorah Emmet Wigoder, describes the circumstances that led a daughter of a devout Catholic family to cross the demarcation line:

> My desire to understand what happened in Germany initiated a systematic study of the Jewish people, tracing their history to biblical times. I realized that the Jews had been persecuted in every era. My father had often explained one of the causes for this. "As long as the Jews refuse to accept the teaching of Christ, they will be persecuted, punished by God and by those men who acknowledge Christ as the Son of God."[9]

Guilt, compassion, and curiosity were only the first step. The decision to become a Jew came to Jane MacDwyer only when she was faced with the new Jewish self-image born in the moments of Israel's birth. She was in the Yiddish theater then, and the leading actor made an announcement: the General Assembly had voted that night, 29 November 1947, to establish a Jewish State:

> Maurice Schwartz had finished talking. Yet no one seemed disposed to leave. The people in the theater were no longer an audience; they constituted one part of a great moment in the biography of the Jewish people. . . .
>
> Looking like Moses, Maurice Schwartz raised his head slightly. Spontaneously the audience rose. How right it seemed—a standing ovation, a tribute to those who made this turning point possible.
>
> But it was more. Beyond the handshake of solidarity, and my compassion for a people injured with alarming regularity, a new image was born. I was conscious of a melody which I tried to place. . . .
>
> Automatically I began to sing. I seemed to be off-key. Waiting for the cue, I was aware of a melodious wave of yearning. This was not a national anthem. What was it then? . . .
>
> Suddenly I understood—the song is a people. Their yearning is mine. Their fate promised to entangle me. Their way of life would be my way of life. Their revelation was an experience I long for.[10]

The Holocaust as starting point, and rebirth as climax, is also the theme of Jan de Hartog's *The Inspector* (1960). The symbol of both is a young Jewess. The protagonist, a non-Jew, comes to grips with himself through participation in both the Holocaust and Jewish rebirth.

Guilt over the Jewish catastrophe and a compulsion to atone prompt a Dutch police inspector to jeopardize career and family, and to smuggle a Jewish survivor of German concentration camps into Palestine. He is Inspector Peter Jongman who, quite by change, comes across a former Nazi on his way from Amsterdam to London escorting a very young, attractive girl. Jongman follows the Nazi criminal and the Jewish victim to London, hoping to have him put under arrest there with the help of Scotland Yard. But the British commander does not cooperate and the Dutchman succeeds merely in getting Anna Held, the Jewess, away from the Nazi. When he finds out from her that the Nazi had contracted, for the exorbitant sum of all her worldly possessions, to take her to Palestine, he inquires:

"And what were you planning to do in Palestine once you got there?" "Become a nurse in a mental hospital for survivors of the camps. It's the only thing that would give me the feeling that everything that has happened to me had a point." Then she added for the first time with some emotion, "I don't think a Christian can realize what Israel means to us. In the camps, we talked about nothing else. . . . Only among Jews can I be myself. Myself, I, and not a generalization: a Jewess among goyim. Now that I am one of the few who survived the camps, I feel even more alien. . . ."[11]

To his and the girl's astonishment, Jongman hears himself offer to smuggle her into British-mandated Palestine. And so begins the Odyssean journey, a path of salvation. For the Gentile this commitment to the Jewess's fervent dream of "Aliyah" is an act of spiritual transformation; for the Jewess it is a flight for life. She is dying. Her body has been mutilated by inhuman experiments in a Nazi research camp, and her health is rapidly declining. Her only hope is to live the last days of her short life in the Jewish land.

The journey is reminiscent of Judith's flight to Zanzibar in the novel by Andersch. Jewish yearning for a haven, security, home, the yearning for an end to fear and alienation are symbolized by both Judith and Anna. The German Andersch and the Dutch Hartog conceived the Jewish agony in similar terms. But there the similarity ends. Judith's flight to Zanzibar, a vague illusory haven, a utopian resting place, is futile and endless. But Anna is fleeing to the Jewish land. It is neither an illusion, nor a utopian paradise: it is a goal and a challenge. And Anna reaches it.

It seems like bitter irony however that Anna reaches Palestine in the last stages of bodily deterioration: she is barely conscious of the great moment. Her emaciated, comatose body is carried ashore by the Dutchman who has endured physical suffering and mental anguish to bring this about. And now, instead of a survivor, he brings a corpse to the Promised Land. Has his triumph turned in the last moment to defeat?

Then the boat hit the gravel of the beach; the boys jumped out and pulled it higher out of the water. He rose precariously: they helped him step out; when he finally stood up to his knees in the water, about to carry her ashore, he looked at the beach and his heart stopped.

For there, with an ominous rattling and the roar of a huge engine, a monster came lumbering out of the night. Steel crunched and screeched on the pebbles as it bore down on them lurching; he realized it was a tank. His first thought was that they had been found out, it must be the British; then the tank swung around and he saw, coarsely chalked on its flank, a Star of David. "Look!" he said. "Anna—look!"

She slowly lifted her head, and looked. For a moment, they seemed to be suspended in a motionless silence, then everything, the night, the sea, the beach, seemed pervaded by her smile.

"Come on! Hurry!" a voice whispered beside him.

He waded ashore toward the tank that stood waiting for her, its engine throbbing. Two of the helmeted boys climbed onto its track, another was waiting in the turret. He carried her to the foot of the tank; then she stretched her thin arms toward it and the boys took her from him. She did not look back; she was lifted up, gently and swiftly, and lowered inside. Then the lid closed, the engine roared, the tank swung around; with a gnashing of steel and pebbles it ground up the slopes of the dunes and rose against the dawn. Its silhouette stood for a moment poised against the sky, angular and grim; then it tipped forward and down, and it was gone, and there was nothing left but the dawn over the hills of Judea.[12]

Holocaust and Rebirth come face to face. Anna, the symbol of the Holocaust, is redeemed after all. Peter Jongman's triumph, poignant and precarious, is undeniably affirmed by "the dawn over the hills of Judea."

Notes

Complete references to the works cited will be found in the Bibliography.

Introduction

1. Eugène Sue, *Le Juif errant,* Epilogue to Part II.
2. Ignoti Monachi Cisterciencis S. Mariae de Ferraria Chronica, 1223 edited by A. Gandenzi, 1888.
3. This version seems to have been the "eye witness" account of an Armenian bishop visiting the monastery of St. Albans recorded by Roger of Wendover, an English monk at the monastery, in his *Flores Historianum* for 1228. Also: Matthew Paris, *Chronica Majora,* 1228 and subsequent annual entries. Also: *Kurtze Beschreibung und Erzehlung von einem Judem mit namen Ahasverus,* 1602, under the imprint of Christoff Kreutzer of Leyden; some copies under the imprint of Wolffgang Suchnach of Bautzen; and of Jakob Rothen of Danzig.
4. Maria Krüger, *Schreiben der Krügerin,* 1756.
5. Avraham Yarmolinsky, *The Wandering Jew; A Contribution toward the Slavonic Bibliogaphy of the Legend,* pp. 324–26. The first tale refers to the Jewess by name: Estya, a Slavic dimunitive of Esther.
6. Genesis 2:18

Chapter 1

1. Jean-Paul Sartre, *Anti-Semite and Jew,* p. 48.
2. *Encyclopedia Judaica,* vol. 15, pp. 150–51.
3. Ibid.
4. Ibid., vol. 6, pp. 907–12.
5. Ibid., vol. 10, pp. 459–62.
6. H. Graetz, *History of the Jews,* vol. II, p. 619; The Expulsion of the Jews from Alexandria by St. Cyril occurred in 415.
7. Ibid., vol. III, p. 76.

8. Yehudit Harari, *Isha V'Em B'Yisrael*, p. 68.
9. The Jewess of Toledo is repeatedly compared to Florinda La Cava, the daughter of Count Julian and the niece of Witiza. According to Castilian legend King Rodrigo, supreme ruler of Spain, abducted her, and, in order to avenge the affront, her father opened the gates of the peninsula to the Moors. The Jewess was blamed for the defeat at Alarcos as she bewitched King Alfonso VIII.
10. Graetz, vol. III, pp. 378–80; Harari, p. 72.
11. S. M. Dubnow, *History of the Jews in Russia and Poland*, vol. I, pp. 53–54; Graetz, IV, p. 122.
12. Harari, p. 73.
13. Graetz, vol. V, pp. 69–70; H. A. Levy, *Sara Copia Sullam*, Berlin, 1862; Harari, pp. 93–94.
14. Harari, p. 95, 98.
15. Graetz, vol. IV, pp. 664–67; Harari, p. 95.
16. Chateaubriand, "Walter Scott et les Juives," *Oeuvres Complète*, vol. XI, pp. 764–66.

Chapter 2

1. Christopher Marlowe, *The Jew of Malta*, Act I, Scene II.
2. Ibid., Act II, Scene III.
3. Montagu F. Modder, *The Jew in the Literature of England: To the end of the 19th century*, pp. 55, 59, 67–69. Charles Lamb, *Essays of Elia* quoted by Malcolm Hay, *Thy Brother's Blood: The Roots of Christian Anti-Semitism*, p. 127.
4. Ibid., p. 125.
5. Marlowe, Act I; Scene I.
6. Ibid., Act II; Scene III.
7. Ibid., Act I; Scene I.
8. Ibid., Act II; Scene III.
9. Ibid., Act III; Scene III.
10. Ibid., Act III; Scene VI.
11. Ibid.
12. Abbé Vacandard, *Études de critique et d'histoire religieuse*, p. 367.
13. Hay, pp. 127–28.
14. Charles Lea, *History of the Inquisition of Spain*, vol. I., p. 134, quoted by Hay, p. 128.
15. Marlowe, Act II; Scene III.

Chapter 3

1. Gotthold E. Lessing, *Nathan the Wise*, p. 135.
2. Montagu F. Modder, *The Jew in the Literature of England*, pp. 55, 59, 67–69.
3. Ibid., p. 56.
4. Abbé Henri Gregoire, *On the Physical, Moral and Political Regeneration of the Jews*, quoted by Howard M. Sachar, *The Course of Modern Jewish History*, p. 55.
5. Modder, pp. 102, 104.

6. Maria Edgeworth, *Harrington,* Chapter 1.
7. Ibid., pp. 80–81.
8. Ibid., p. 203.
9. Ibid., p. 81.
10. Anna M. Porter, *The Village of Mariendorpt,* p. 130.

Chapter 4

1. Walter Scott, *Ivanhoe,* p. 232.
2. George du Maurier, *The Martian,* p. 140.
3. Scott, p. 231.
4. William M. Thackeray, *Rebecca and Rowena,* p. 3.
5. Quoted by Modder, p. 375.
6. Herman Melville, *Clarel: A Poem and Pilgrimage in the Holy Land,* pp. 55–56.
7. Ibid., p. 125.
8. Ibid., p. 513.
9. Anton Chekhov, *Ivanov,* pp. 15, 17.

Chapter 5

1. Jean-Paul Sartre, *Anti-Semite and Jew,* p. 48–49.
2. Honoré de Balzac, *A Harlot High and Low,* pp. 41–42.
3. Guy de Maupassant, *Mademoiselle Fifi and Other Stories.*
4. Henry Adams, *Mont-Saint-Michel and Chartres,* p. 191.
5. Ibid., pp. 272–73.
6. René de Chateaubriand, *Memoires.*
7. Victor Hugo, "La Sultane Favorite," *Les Orientales,* pp. 142–45.
8. Adams, pp. 265–66.
9. Ibid., pp. 263–64.
10. In *La Maison Tellier* where "she fulfilled the indispensable role of the belle Juive"; just as did Vanda in J. K. Huysmans, *À rebours* (1903), p. 161.
11. Adams, p. 266.
12. Leon Daudet, *Ceux qui montent,* p. 14.
13. Balzac, pp. 28–30.
14. Ibid., pp. 55–56.
15. Ibid., pp. 56–57.
16. Algernon Charles Swinburne, "Dolores, Our Lady of Pain," in *Poetry of the Victorian Period,* ed. by G. B. Woods and J. H. Buckley.
17. Quoted by Sol Liptzin, *The Jew in American Literature,* pp. 53–57.

Chapter 6

1. Mme. Rattazzi, *La Belle Juive,* p. 5.
2. Enacryos, *La Juive,* p. 7.
3. Quoted in *Encyclopedia of Zionism and Israel,* vol. 1, p. 350.
4. Ibid., p. 351.
5. A. Leroy-Beaulieu, *Israel chez les nations,* p. 333.
6. A. Dreyfus, "Le Juif au Théâtre," *Revue des Etudes Juives,* V, 49.

7. Alexandre Dumas, fils, *La Femme de Claude,* p. 168.
8. Paul Bourget, *Cosmopolis,* p. 6.
9. Walter Besant, *The Rebel Queen,* p. 5.
10. Ibid., p. 4.

Chapter 7

1. Alexander Sholokhov, *And Quiet Flows the Don,* p. 392.
2. Ibid., pp. 392–93.
3. J.-P. Sartre, *Anti-Semite and the Jew,* pp. 86–87.
4. Ibid., pp. 87–88.
5. Quoted by Hay, p. 177.
6. Adolf Hitler, *Mein Kampf,* p. 65.
7. *Le Monde,* 6 May 1886, quoted by Hay, *op cit.,* p. 180.
8. 13 May 1866
9. The Jews comprised one-quarter of one percent of France's population.
10. Quoted by Hay, p. 181.
11. Ibid., p. 182.
12. L. Psenner, *Oesterr. Volksfreund,* 31 May 1886.
13. Hay, p. 200.
14. *Trial of the Major War Criminals,* XVIII, p. 197.
15. Ernest Renan, *Etudes d'histoire religieuse,* pp. 86–89; quoted by Raphael Patai, *Myth of the Jewish Race,* p. 10.
16. Richard Wagner, *Das Judenthum in der Musik;* as quoted by W. Keller, *Diaspora: The Post-Biblical History of the Jews,* p. 415.
17. Houston S. Chamberlain, *The Foundations of the Nineteenth Century.*

Chapter 8

1. Pearl S. Buck, *The Bondmaid,* p. 312.
2. Henry Feingold, *Zion in America,* pp. 273–76.
3. Thomas Wolfe, *The Web and the Rock,* p. 547.
4. James Michener, *The Source,* p. 47.
5. Ibid., p. 13.
6. Ibid., pp. 78–79.
7. Ibid., pp. 82–83.
8. Ibid., p. 83.
9. Devorah Wigoder, *Hope Is My House,* p. 61.
10. Ibid., pp. 72–73.
11. Jan de Hartog, *The Inspector,* pp. 46–47.
12. Ibid., pp. 311–12.

Bibliography

Historical and Literary References

Abrahams, Israel. " 'The Deacon and the Jewess,' Prefatory Notes." *Transactions of the Jewish Historical Society of England, vol. 6, p.254.*

—— *Jewish Life in the Middle Ages.* Philadelphia: Jewish Publication Society of America, 1961.

Adams, Henry. *Mont-Saint-Michel and Chartres.* New York: The New American Library, 1961.

Anderson, George, K. *The Legend of the Wandering Jew.* Providence: Brown University Press, 1965.

Barzilay, Isaac. "The Jew in the Literature of the Enlightenment." *Jewish Social Studies,* vol. 18 (October 1956): 243.

Beard, Mary R. *Woman as Force in History: A Study in Traditions and Realities.* New York: The Macmillan Company, 1946.

Bloch, Maurice. "The Jewish Woman in German, English, and French Novel." *Revue des Études Juives,* 23 (1891).

Bloch, Maurice. "La femme Juive dans le roman et au théâtre." *Revue des Études Juives,* 24 (1892).

Bob, Julius. "Shylock-Nathan-Judith." *Der Morgen,* 1, no. 2 (1925): 209–25.

Byrnes, R. F. "Edouard Drumont and *La France Juive.*" *Jewish Social Studies,* 10, no. 2 (April 1948): 165.

Cansinos-Assens, Rafael. *Los Judĭos en la Literatura Española.* Buenos Aires, 1937.

Carrington, Herbert de Witt. *Die Figur des Juden in der dramatischen Literatur des XVIII. Jahrhunderts.* Heidelberg, 1897.

Coleman, Edward D. "Jewish Prototypes in American and English Novels and Mysteries, 1634–1936." *American Jewish Historical Society Publications,* no. 35.

Comtet, Maurice. *"V. G. Korolenko et la Question Juive en Russie."* *École Practique des Hautes Études, Sorbonne,* Sixieme Section: Sciences Sociales, 10 (1969).

Debré, Moses. *The Image of the Jew in French Literature from 1800 to 1908.* Translated by Gertrude Hirschler. New York: Ktav Publishing House, 1970.

Dejob, Charles. "Le Juif dans la comédie aux XIIIe siècle." *Revue des Études Juives,* 34 (1899); 119–28.

Dreyfus, Abraham. "Le Juif au théâtre." *Revue des Études Juives,* 5 (1886): 49.

Dubnow, Simon M. *History of the Jews in Russia and Poland.* 3 vols. New York: Ktav Publishing House, 1975.

Encyclopedia Judaica, New York: The Macmillan Company, 1971.

Feingold, Henry. *Zion in America.* New York: Twayne Publishers, 1974.

Frankl, Oskar. "Die Jüdin in der deutschen Dichtung." *Die Welt,* 16, no. 13 (1912): 408–11.

Geiger, Ludwig. *Die deutsche Literatur und die Juden.* Berlin, 1910.

Gomez de Salazar, J. "Alphonse VIII de Doña Fermosa." *Evidences,* no. 22 (December 1951).

Graetz, Heinrich H. *History of the Jews.* 6 vols. Philadelphia: The Jewish Publication Society of America, 1893.

—— *Shylock in der Sage, in Drama und in der Geschichte.* Krotoschin, 1880.

Grossman, Rudolph. "The Jew in Novels." *American Hebrew,* 50 (1892): 122–23.

Harari, Yehudit. *Isha V'Em B'Yisrael.* Tel Aviv: Massada, 1959.

Hay, Malcolm. *Thy Brother's Blood: The Roots of Christian Anti-Semitism.* New York: Hart Publishing Co., 1975.

Jacobowski, Ludwig. "Jüdische Stoffe in der Moderner Dichtung." *Jüdisches Literatur-Blatt,* 20 (1891): 148–49.

Isaac, Jules. *The Teaching of Contempt: Christian Roots of Anti-Semitism.* New York and Toronto: Holt & Rinehart, 1964.

Jung, Gustav. *Die Darstellung des Weibes in Heinrich Heines Werken.* Leipzig, 1879.

Keller, Werner. *Diaspora: The Post-Biblical History of the Jews.* New York: Harcourt Brace, 1969.

Kayserling, M. *Die jüdische Frauen in der Geschichte, Literatur und Kunst.* Leipzig, 1879.

Kunitz, Joshua. *Russian Literature and the Jew: A Sociological Inquiry into the Nature and Origin of Literary Patterns.* New York: Columbia University Press, 1929.

Landa, M. J. *The Jew in Drama.* New York, 1927.

Lea, Charles. *History of the Inquisition of Spain.* New York, 1906–07.

Leroy-Beaulieu, Anatole. *Israel chez les Nations.* Paris: Calman-Levy, 1893.

Lifschitz-Golden, Manya. *Les Juifs dans la littérature française du moyen age.* New York, 1935.

Liptzin, Sol. *The Jew in American Literature.* New York: Bloch Publishing Co., 1966.

Loeb, Isidore. *Le Juif de l'histoire et de la legende.* Paris, 1889.

Lublinsky, S. *Judische Charactere bei Grillparzer, Hebbel und Otto Ludwig.* Berlin, 1899.

Mabon, Doris. "The Jew in Fiction." *Jewish Chronicle Supplement* (June 1929).

Mersand, Joseph. *Traditions in American Literature: A Study of Jewish Characters and Authors.* New York: Modern Chapbeohs, 1939.

Meyer, Wilhelm. *Der Wandel des judischen Typus in der englischen Literatur.* Inaugural-Dissertation, University of Marburg, 1912.

Michelson, Hijman. *The Jew in Early English Literature.* Amsterdam, 1926.

Modder, Montagu Frank. *The Jew in the Literature of England: To the end of the 19th century.* Cleveland and New York: Meridian Books; Philadelphia: The Jewish Publication Society of America, 1961.

Mosse, Goerge Lachman. "The Image of the Jew in German Popular Culture: Felix Dahn and Gustav Freytag." *Leo Baeck Institute Yearbook,* 2 (1957): 218.

Patai, Raphael and Wing, Jennifer. *The Myth of the Jewish Race.* New York: Charles Scribner's Sons, 1975.

Parkes, James W. *The Jew and His Neighbor; a Study of the Causes of Anti-Semitism.* London, 1931.
Philipson, David. *The Jew in English Fiction.* Cincinnati, 1889.
Poliakov, Leon. *The History of Anti-Semitism,* vol. 3. New York: Vanguard, 1975.
Purdie, Edna. *The Story of Judith in German and English Literature. Bibliotheque de la Revue de littèrature comparèe,* tome 39.
Randall, Earle Stanley. *The Jewish Character in the French Novel 1870–1914.* Doctoral Dissertation. Menasha, Wis., 1941.
Sachar, Howard Morley. *The Course of Modern Jewish History.* New York: Dell Publishing Co., 1958.
Stern, Selma. "Die Entwicklung des jüdischen Frauentypus." *Der Morgen,* 1 (1925): 324–37.
Scheiber, Alexander. "The Legend of the Wandering Jew in Hungary." *Midwest Folklore,* 4 (1954): 221–35 and 6 (1956): 155–58.
Schwartz, M. "Dostoyevsky and Judaism." *Jewish Review,* no. 4 (April-June 1933): 57–63.
Schwartz, Rudolph. *Esther in deutschen und neulateinischen Drama des Reformationsalter.* Odenburg-Leipzig, 1898.
Schweitzer, Jerome. "The Jewess of Toledo: Three Unstudied Dramatic Adaptations of the Raquel-Alphonso VIII Legend." *Romance Notes,* no. 1 (1962): 21.
The Universal Jewish Encyclopedia. 10 vols. New York: Universal Jewish Encyclopedia Co., 1942.
Vacandard, Elphège. *Études de critique et d'histoire religieuse,* 3rd series. Paris, 1912.
Wachstein, Bernhard. *Literatur über die jüdische Frau.* Wien, 1931.
Wallerstein, David. "The Jew in Fiction." *The Jewish Exponent,* 1 (1887): 4.
Weiss, Trude Rosmarin. *Jewish Woman through the Ages.* New York: Jewish Peoples' Library, 1940.
Yarmolinsky, Avraham. *The Wandering Jew; A Contribution toward the Slavonic Bibliography of the Legend.* Vanguard Press, 1929.
Zirus, Werner. *Der ewige Jude in der Dichtung; vornehmlich in der englischen und deutschen.* Leipzig, 1928.

Literary Works with Jewish Subjects

Andersch, Alfred. *Sansibar oder der letzte Grund.* Berlin, 1965.
Balzac, Honoré de. *Gobseck.* Paris, 1842.
——— *La Maison Nucingen.* Paris, 1847.
——— *A Harlot High and Low.* New York: Penguin Books, 1970.
Becquer, Gustavo Adolfo. *La Rosa de Pasion: Rimas y leyendas.* Buenos Aires, 1969.
Besant, Walter. *The Rebel Queen.* New York: Harper and Bros., 1893.
Blessington, Countess of. *The Jew's Daughter.* London, 1840.
Bonnières, Robert de. *Les Monachs.* Paris, 1885.
Bourget, Paul. *Cosmopolis.* Paris, 1892.
Brandes, Johann Christian. *Rahel, die Schöne Jüdinn.* Sämmtliche dramatische Schriften, Hamburg, 1790–91.
Brecht, Bertold. "Die Judische Frau:" *Furcht und Elend des dritten Reiches,* Berlin, 1934–37.
Bristow, Amalia. *Sophia de Lisseau.* London, 1840.

Brown, Charles Brockden. *Arthur Mervyn.* New York: Holt, Rinehart and Winston, 1979.

Brown, Claude. *Manchild in the Promised Land.* New York: The Macmillan Company, 1966.

Buck, Pearl S. *The Bondmaid.* New York: J. Day Co., 1949.

Bulwer, Edward, Lord Lytton. *Leila; or the Siege of Granada.* London: George Rutledge and Sons, 1875.

Byron, George, Lord Gordon. "Hebrew Melodies; Jephtah's Daughter; She Walks in Beauty; Herod's Lament for Marianne; By the Rivers of Babylon . . ." *The Complete Poetical Works of Lord Byron.* Boston: Houghton Mifflin, 1946.

Cazotte, Jaques. *Rachel, où la belle Juive.* Paris, 1778.

Cèline, Louis-Ferdinand. *Bagatelles pour un massacre.* Paris, 1937.

—— *Ecole des cadavres.* Paris, 1938.

—— *Voyage au bout de la nuit.* Paris, 1932.

Chamberlain, Houston S. *Die Grundlagen des neuzehnten Jahrhunderts.* Berlin, 1898.

Chateaubriand, François René de. *"Walter Scott et les Juives," Oeuvres Completes,* vol. 11, pp. 764–66. Paris, 1861.

Chaucer, Geoffrey. *The Canterbury Tales.* New York: Holt, Rinehart and Winston, 1929.

Chekhov, Anton. *Ivanov.* New York: Holt, Rinehart and Winston, 1916.

Chevalier, P. E. *Rachel, où la belle Juive.* Paris, 1803.

Chirikov, Evgenii N. *The Jews.* Moscow, 1904.

Corneille, Pierre. *Tite et Bērénice.* Paris, 1670.

Cumberland, Richard. *The Jew.* London, 1794.

—— *The Fashionable Lover.* London, 1772.

Dahn, Felix. *Ein Kampf um Rom.* Leipzig, 1904.

Daudet, Leon. *Ceux qui montent.* Paris, 1912.

Dickens, Charles. *Oliver Twist.* New York: World Publishers, 1941.

Diego, V. Garcia de. "La Judia Raquel," *Antologia de Leyendas.* Madrid, 1953.

Disraeli, Benjamin. *Conigsby; or the New Generation.* The Brandenham Edition of the Novels and Tales of Benjamin Disraeli, 1st Earl of Beaconsfield, vol. 8. New York: Alfred A. Knopf, 1934.

—— *Tancred.* New York: Alfred A. Knopf, 1934.

Donnay, Maurice. *Le Retour de Jerusalem.* Paris, 1903.

Donnely, Ignatius. *Caesar's Column, a Story of the Twentieth Century.* Chicago, 1891.

Dostoyevskii, F. M. *House of the Dead.* London: Nelson, Foster & Scott, 1958.

Doyle, Conan. "A Scandal in Bohemia." *The Complete Sherlock Holmes.* New York: Doubleday, 1930.

Dreiser, Theodore. *The Hand of the Potter.* New York, 1918.

Edgeworth, Maria. *Tales and Novels*, vol. 9. London: H. G. Bohn and Simpkin, Marshall, and Co., 1870.

Eliot, George. *Daniel Deronda.* The Personal Edition of George Eliot's Works. New York: Doubleday, Page & Co., 1901.

Enacryos (pseud. of C. J. Rosny-Aine). *La Juive.* Paris, 1907.

Erckmann, Emile and Chatrian, Alexandre. *L'Ami Fritz.* Paris, 1864.

Flaubert, Gustave. *Herodias.* London: Hacon & Rickets, 1901.

Ford, Paul L. *Janice Meredith; A Story of the American Revolution.* New York, 1899.

Franzos, Karl Emil. *Judith Trachtenberg.* Breslau, 1819.

Freytag, Gustav. *Soll und Haben.* Regensburg, 1928.

Frisch, Max. *Andorra.* Stücke, vol. 2. Frankfurt, 1962.
Gellert, Christian F. *Briefe der schwedischen Grafin von G.* Bern, 1767–76.
Gobineau, J. Arthur de. *Essai sur l'inégalité des races humaines.* Paris, 1855.
Gogol, Nikolai. *Taras Bulba.* New York, 1886.
Goncourt, Edmond et Jules de. *Manette Salomon.* Paris, 1833.
Gorkii, Maxim. "The Jewish Massacre." Vienna-Leipzig, 1904.
Grillparzer, Franz. *Die Jüdin von Toledo.* Yarmouth Port, 1953.
Gutzkow, Karl. "Die ewige Jüdin." *Schönere Stunden.* Stuttgart, 1869.
Hardung, Victor. *Ahasvera.* Berlin, 1895.
Harland, Henry. *Mrs. Peixada.* New York, 1886.
Hartog, Jan de. *The Inspector.* New York: Atheneum Publishers, 1960.
Hauptmann, Hans. *Memoiren des Satans.* Munich, 1929.
Hauschner, Auguste. *Familie Losowitz.* Berlin, 1908.
Haushofer, Max. *Der ewige Jude.* Leipzig, 1886.
Hebbel, Friedrich. *Judith; eine Tragödie in fünf Akten.* Frankfurt, 1966.
Hawthorne, Nathaniel. *The Marble Faun.* New York: The Bobbs-Merrill Co., 1971.
Hermann, George. *Jettchen Gebert.* Berlin, 1931.
—— *Henriette Jacoby.* Berlin, 1908.
Heywood, Joseph C. *Salome: A Dramatic Poem.* New York, 1867.
Hitler, Adolf. *Mein Kampf.* Translated by Ralph Manheim. Boston: Houghton Mifflin Co., 1943.
Holbach, Franz. *Kamerad Levy.* Berlin, 1921.
Hugo, Victor. "La Sultane Favorite." *Les Orientales.* Paris, 1833.
Huysmans, J. K. *À rebours.* Paris, 1903.
Huerta, Vicente A. Gracia de la. *LaRaquel.* Madrid: Classicos Castalia, 1971.
Jünger, Nathaniel. *Volk in Gefahr.* Berlin, 1921.
Kahlenberg, Hans von. *Ahasvera.* Berlin, 1910.
Kotzebue, August F. *Kind der Liebe.* Leipzig, 1791.
Krüger, Maria. *Schreiben der Krügerin.* Halle-Halmstedt, 1756.
Kuffner, Christoff. *Die ewige Judin und der Orang-Utan.* Vienna, 1846.
Kukolnik, Nestor V. *The Statue of Christoph in Riga.* St. Petersburg, 1852.
—— *Prince Daniel Vasilievich Kholmskii.* St. Petersburg, 1852.
Kuprin, Alexander. "The Jewess." *Bracelet of Garnets and Other Stories.* New York: Charles Scribner's Sons, 1917.
Lazhechnikov, Ivan. *Daughter of the Jew.* St. Petersburg, 1849.
Lermontov, M. Y. "Hebrew Melodies." "Whither so fast, Young Jewess?" *Sobranie Sochinenii,* vol. 1. Moscow, 1957.
—— *The Spaniards. Sobranie Sochinenii,* vol. 7. Moscow, 1957.
Lessing, Gotthold E. *Nathan der Weise.* Leipzig, 1855.
Lotich, Johann K. *Wer war wohl mehr Jude?* Leipzig, 1783.
Luther, Martin. *Of the Jews and Their Lies.* 1543.
Malamud, Bernard. *The Assistant.* New York: The American Library, 1957.
Marlowe, Christopher. *The Jew of Malta.* New York: Hill and Wang, 1966.
Marr, Wilhelm. *Der Sieg des Judentums über das Germanentums.* Berlin, 1879.
Maupassant, Guy de. *Mademoiselle Fifi, Parisian Adventure, and Other Stories.* New York: Stravon, 1949.
Melville, Herman. *Clarel. A Poem and Pilgrimage in the Holy Land.* New York: Hendricks House, 1930.
Merville, Pierre Francois C. and Maillan, J. de. *Le Juif Errant.* Paris, 1834.

Metastasio, Pietro. *La clemenza di Tito.* Rome, 1777.
Michener, James. *The Source.* New York: Random House, 1965; New York: Fawcett Crest.
Montchretien, Antoine. *Esther.* Paris, 1585.
Mühsam, Paul. "Der ewige Jude." Leipzig, 1924.
Nietzsche, Friedrich. *Beyond Good and Evil.* London, 1967.
—— *The Geneology of Morals.* New York, 1964.
Otway, Thomas. *Titus and Berenice.* London, 1677.
Pfeffel, Gottlieb Conrad. "Alfons und Rahel." *Poetische Versuche,* vol. 7. gen, bingen, 1804.
Polenz, Wilhelm von. *Der Büttnerbauer.* Berlin, 1906.
Porter, Anna Maria. *The Village of Mariendorpt,* vol. 1. London, 1821.
Puente, Lazaro Montero de la. *Doña Fermosa.* Madrid, 1955.
Pushkin, Alexander S. "The Black Shawl." "The Avaricious Knight." "Christ is Risen, Oh My Rebekka!" "Judith." *The Works of A. Pushkin.* New York: Random House, 1936.
Quinet, Edgar. *Ahasverus.* Paris, 1833.
Raabe, Wilhelm. *Der Hungerpastor.* Berlin, 1862.
Rattazzi, Mme. (Maria Letizia Bonaparte-Wyse). *La Belle Juive: Episode du Siege de Jerusalem.* Paris, 1882.
Renan, Ernest. *Etudes d'histoire religieuse.* Paris, Michel Levy Frères: 1862.
Rohling, August. *Der Talmudjude.* Prague, 1875.
Sartre, Jean-Paaul. *Anti-Semite and Jew.* New York: Schocken Books, 1948.
Savoir, Alfred and Nozière. *Le Baptème.* Paris, 1907.
Schnitzler, Arthur. *Weg ins Freie. Gesammelte Werke.* Frankfurt, 1961.
Schonneaus, Cornelius. *Juditha,* 1574.
Scott, Walter. *Ivanhoe.* London: The Macmillan Co., 1926.
Shakespeare, William. *The Merchant of Venice.* New York: Simon and Schuster, 1957.
Sheridan, Richard Brinsley. *The Duenna.* London, 1775.
—— *The School for Scandal.* London, 1977.
Sholokhov, Mikhail A. *And Quiet Flows the Don.* New York: Alfred A. Knopf, 1959.
Smollett, Tobias. *The Adventures of Count Fathom.* London, 1753.
—— *The Adventures of Roderick Random.* London, 1748.
Steinberg, Karl. *Menschen und Menschensituationen.* Frankfurt u. Leipzig, 1787.
Sue, Eugène. *Le Juif errant.* Paris, 1844-5.
Swinburne, Algernon Charles. "Dolores, Our Lady of Pain." *Poetry of the Victorian Period.* Edited by G. B. Woods and J. H. Buckley. New York: Scott-Foresman and Co., 1955.
Thackeray, William M. *Rebecca and Rowena.* Boston, 1901.
Tressera, Ceferino. *La Judia Errante.* Madrid, 1862.
Turgenev, Ivan S. "Hapless Girl." "The Jew." *The Jew and Other Stories.* New York: Charles Scribner's Sons, 1904.
Updike, John. *Bech: A Book.* New York: Alfred A. Knopf, 1970.
Vidal, Gore. *Washington, D. C.* Boston: Little, Brown & Co., 1962
Viereck, George S. and Eldridge, Paul. *Salome... My First Two Thousand Years of Love.* New York: Liveright, 1931.
Wade, Thomas. *The Jew of Arragon, or the Hebrew Queen.* London, 1830.
Wagner, Richard. *Das Judenthum in der Musik* (Jewry in Music). Leipzig: J. J. Weber, 1869.

Walling, Günther (pseud. Karl Ulrici). "Rahel von Toledo." *Von Lenz zu Herbst: Dichtungen.* Berlin: Leipzig University, 1887.
Wigoder, Devorah. *Hope Is My House.* New York: Prentice Hall, 1966.
Wolfe, Thomas. *Of Time and River.* New York: Charles Scribner's Sons, 1935.
—— *The Web and the Rock.* New York: Harper and Bros., 1938.
—— *You Can't Go Home Again.* New York and London: Harper and Bros., 1940.